Chronicle of an Impossible Election

Chronicle of an Impossible Election

The Election Commission and the 2002 Jammu and Kashmir Assembly Elections

JAMES MICHAEL LYNGDOH

PENGUIN
VIKING

VIKING
Published by the Penguin Group
Penguin Books India Pvt Ltd, 11 Community Centre, Panchsheel Park,
New Delhi 110 017, India
Penguin Group (USA) Inc., 375 Hudson Street, New York,
New York 10014, USA
Penguin Group (Canada), 10 Alcorn Avenue, Toronto, Ontario,
Canada M4V 3B2 (a division of Pearson Penguin Canada Inc.)
Penguin Books Ltd, 80 Strand, London WC2R 0RL, England
Penguin Ireland, 25 St Stephen's Green, Dublin 2, Ireland
(a division of Penguin Books Ltd)
Penguin Group (Australia), 250 Camberwell Road, Camberwell,
Victoria 3124, Australia (a division of Pearson Australia Group Pty Ltd)
Penguin Group (NZ), cnr Airborne and Rosedale Roads, Albany,
Auckland 1310, New Zealand (a division of Pearson New Zealand Ltd)
Penguin Group (South Africa) (Pty) Ltd, 24 Sturdee Avenue, Rosebank,
Johannesburg 2196, South Africa

Penguin Books Ltd, Registered Offices: 80 Strand, London WC2R 0RL, England

First published in Viking by Penguin Books India 2004

Copyright © James Michael Lyngdoh 2004

All rights reserved

10 9 8 7 6 5 4 3 2 1

The views and opinions expressed in this book are the author's own and the facts
are as reported by him which have been verified to the extent possible, and the
publishers are not in any way liable for the same.

Typeset in Sabon Roman by SÜRYA, New Delhi
Printed at Saurabh Printers Pvt. Ltd., Noida

Contents

Preface

A book of this kind is, at the very least, a useful chronicle of the Jammu and Kashmir elections, 2002, even if about two years too old, the reason being it was not right for me to bring it out while in service.

Quite honestly these elections had been at once so thrilling and exhausting that when David Davidar, Chief Executive Officer and Publisher, Penguin Books India, lobbed a stone into my after-it-was-all-over catharsis and asked me to write about them, I barely agreed.

Obviously, the effort could not be a mere account of the elections, much less a Te Deum to the Election Commission without root or context. So some recent history of the state has had to be added. The Election Commission had been inseparably bound to elections in the state and has also had to figure. But I soon ran into the reality of the contradiction of an Election Commission otherwise held in high regard but seen in Jammu and Kashmir only as a tool of the Government of India. In handling this contradiction I have had to devote more than a third of the book to the Election Commission per se.

The elections themselves, a web of inter-related events from well before the polling till long after it, retrospecting, meant the stupendous task of recalling details and putting them together. Chronologically, of course, as this was the only way they made sense and lighted up the whole.

The Election Commission made seven visits and these provided the milestones to the chapterization of the book. Deputy Election Commissioners Sayan Chatterjee and Ajay Jha, Legal Counsel Surinder Mendiratta, Consultant Kommajosyula Rao, Chief Electoral Officer, Uttar Pradesh Noor Mohammad and Chief Electoral Officer, Punjab, Gurjit Cheema needed not only to re-focus on matters they had been delighted to leave behind but to even write notes to revive the events. As participant and scribe, I am indebted to all of them for the part they have played in the elections, for their notes and suggestions to the bitter end of this opus. As well as to Private Secretary Thamby Jeyaraj and UDCs Raj Kumar and Awadhesh Kumar for resolving many a confusion and patiently putting this book to type.

I have added a bibliography but have borrowed so much from Justice A.S. Anand's *The Constitution of Jammu and Kashmir* (Chapters 2 and 3), Surinder Mendiratta's *How India Votes, Election Laws, Practice And Procedure* (Chapters 7 to 16), M.J. Akbar's *Kashmir: Behind the Vale* (Chapters 2 and 4) and Fida Hassnains's *A Search for the Historical Jesus* (Chapter 2) that I need to acknowledge this separately.

I am grateful to David Davidar for commissioning me for what has eventually turned out to be a very pleasant and satisfying work. Also to Krishan Chopra, Managing Editor, who always cast the shadow of a whip across my long spells of indolence.

Finally, an acknowledgement to my wife, Parveen for sitting out the torment of taking down dictation in longhand between dinner and bedtime in midsummer, making sense out of a lot of nonsense and tidying the book to its present coherence.

Hyderabad   **J.M. Lyngdoh**
15 April 2004

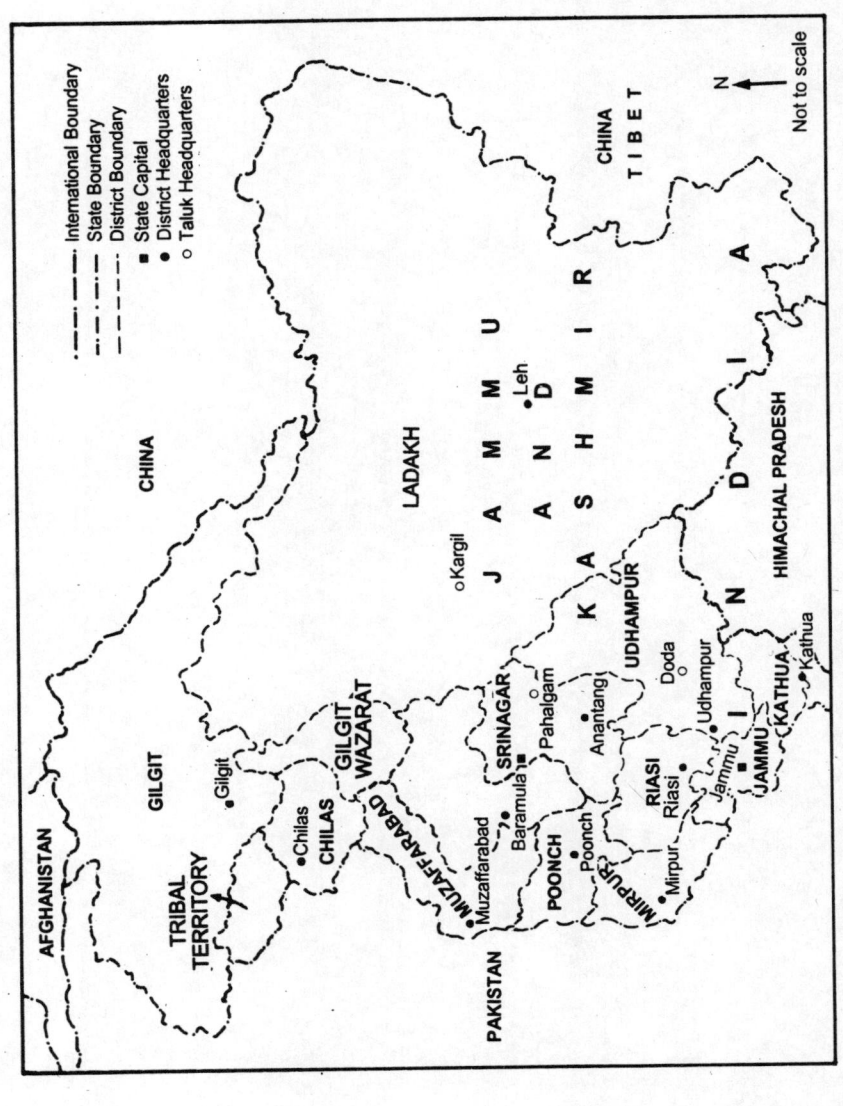

Part One

Scepticism in the Light . . .

A credible election in Jammu and Kashmir in September, 2002 seemed unachievable, much less a 'free and fair' election as they call it in India, however lightly the cliché trips over the tongue. The Indian and Pakistani armies had had a long political face-off on the international border and civil order inside the state, so dependent on the Indian soldier, had visibly slackened. And Pakistan, once again quite sated with the ecstasies of military rule, was looking forward even to a transparently ersatz general election in which civilian powers had been docked to keep the army in control. How convenient therefore for Pakistan to see a still more depreciated election in Jammu and Kashmir. And how easy for them to manipulate one.

But there were more serious reasons. Though the predominantly Hindu and Buddhist residents of the Jammu and Ladakh regions respectively had felicitously cohered with India, the overwhelmingly Muslim population of the Kashmir Valley—and overall, Muslims were still in the majority—still chafed with neither having the freedom to determine their own future nor autonomy. Even worse, they saw themselves as often not having had a government they could call their own either because it was manipulated or the elections were not fair. Which also meant that the Election Commission of India was yet indistinguishable from the Government of India. Moreover, the matter was not limited to adverse Kashmiri perceptions. The Western media had been by and large anti-Indian over Kashmir and alleged human rights violations by security forces had only made it more acerbic. Even otherwise India, over the years, had peeved the West with non-alignment and what was seen as preachy self-righteousness. More recently, India had liberalized too slowly for the patience of Western capitalism. Not that Indians were easy to do business with, Transparency International's corruption perception index for India being among the highest in the world. Most of this needs elaboration.

Of History

The Kashmir problem was intrinsically one of an uncommonly cerebral people, extremely sensitive, very conscious of their identity as an ancient, distinct race inhabiting the paradisal vale of Kashmir, enduringly proud of their past but consumed with anger at what they perceived as successive subjections to a variety of contemptuous rulers (most books on Kashmir splurged colourful but coloured quotations about the Kashmiri character), as well as a persistent indignation over hundreds of years at their own defensive prevarication.

But what was the Kashmiri's historical perspective? There is compelling evidence that Kashmiris are descended from the Kassite or Kash tribe—hence Kasheer or Kashmir—or the Biblical Kush, after Noah's grandson, Kush. (The important tribes before them in the Valley had been the Nagas, Pishachis, Gandharas and Turganas.) And similarities between Jews and Kashmiris have persisted. For example, graves are arranged east to west; coffins have a pointed top; the period of mourning is forty days; smoked fish is a common meal; koshered meat has always been de rigueur; birth, marriage and death rites are identical; 9 per cent of Kashmiri still consists of Hebrew words.

Apocryphal, Sanskrit, Buddhist and Islamic sources together showed that between his thirteenth and twenty-seventh years Jesus, who was an Essene—Essenes, a sect among the Jews as distinct from the Pharisees and Sadducees, were noted for their poverty, honesty, justice and equality—travelled from Mesopotamia to Iran, Sind, Uttar Pradesh (Varanasi), Orissa (Puri) and Nepal (Kapilavastu). He was six years in a Buddhist monastery and imbibed so much of Buddhism as to be considered an Arhat. And he was thought to have transmitted much of Buddhism to Christianity, for example, celibate monks and nuns and the concepts of the trinity and of offering the other cheek to one who had struck you on one cheek. Returned to his homeland and ever defiant of orthodoxy, he was crucified. But since he soon attained samadhi and appeared dead to the uninitiated he was allowed to be removed from the cross. The Essenes treated his wounds with spices and salves and laid him in a grotto. It was there that he recovered. Obliged to distance himself from his enemies, he with his mother again took to the east—Iran, Central Asia, Punjab (Taxila) and Kashmir (Srinagar), where he was eventually buried. Jesus' grave, which also had a wooden sepulchre, was known as the shrine of Yusu Asaph of Rosabal. Mary's grave was in the neighbouring Pakistani hill resort of Murree (derived from Mary). Much older, Moses' grave on the hill of Nabu in Bethpor was known as the shrine of the 'Prophet of the Book'. And lying at the feet of the hill of Nabu, the Valley, scripturally—most of the place names in the Bible matching with those in that part of Kashmir—topographically and ecologically, out of all places on earth, best exemplified the promised land of the Bible. Evidently the Kashmiris were one of the ten lost tribes of Israel.

As part of the Jewish diaspora from Mesopotamia to

Kashmir, the Kashmiris were not rigid about religion and changed with the wind. They became Hindus—Emperor Ashoka, prior to his conversion, founded the city of Srinagar—and then turned to Buddhism. The third century Buddhist Conference in Kashmir, in the reign of Kanishka, saw the birth of Mahayana Buddhism. Kashmir, the only part of the subcontinent with four distinct seasons and a natural apprehension of seasonal symbols, had always been strongly Saivite, appreciating the trinity of Shiva the destroyer, Durga the creator and Parvati the preserver. It was Kashmiri Saivism which gave to esoteric Hinayana Buddhism—in which each individual had to work out his own deliverance from suffering—a comfortable, anthropomorphic divine order composed of Shiva the Supreme Being and of the gods and goddesses of the cult who could be manipulated for private purposes. The orientation of Buddhism towards society promoted the Bodhisattva, the person who, instead of striving for his own salvation, stayed on in the world to show to others the way of attaining the blessings of the Dhamma. As Buddhism lost ground in the subcontinent monistic Saivism, peculiar to the Valley in the eighth century, accelerated a return to Hinduism. Finally, there was an almost complete conversion—barring rather more than half the Pandits—to Sufi—mystical—Islam. The native Saivism had threaded through so many faiths, accounting for the Kashmiris' catholic sensibilities and secular inclinations—in the Indian sense of being even-handed with all religions. Their greatest Muslim king, Zainul Abidin—the first to throw a wooden bridge (Zainakadal) over the Jhelum, and an enthusiastic patron of the arts, especially music—had even erred in favour of the minority, having abolished *jiziya* and cow slaughter and restored *sati*.

The Kashmiri had much more to proudly retrospect

upon. In pre-Islamic times, King Avantivarmana (Avantipur, an imperial headquarters with the ruins of capital temples and palaces named after him) had the course of the Jhelum changed to drain a vast area for agriculture.

And King Lalitaditya had extended his kingdom to Tibet, Badakshan, Punjab and Uttar Pradesh up to Kanauj. About him the poet Kalhan, in his *Rajatarangini**—literally, the river of kings—had said:

> Then the illustrious King Lalitaditya became the universal monarch, he who was [far] beyond the conception of Fate which creates [only] rulers of limited territories.

> With the shining mass of his glory's rays he adorned, as it were, the elephant [representing the isle] of Jambudvipa with scented powders.

> This king, who carried far his prowess, abandoned his [warlike] fury [only] when the [opposing] kings discreetly folded their palms at his victorious onset.

> At the sound of his drums [beaten] in attack, the dwellings of his enemies were deserted by the [frightened] inhabitants, and thus resembled women dropping in fright the burden of their wombs.

> He made the enemies' wives, on whose faces the ends of the [painted] forehead-marks became detached, and whose tears were flowing, perform, as it were, oblations to the Pitrs [nivapa] with folded hands.

---

* *Kalhana's Rajatarangini—A Chronicle of the Kings of Kashmir,* Vol. 1, by M.A. Stein (Motilal Banarsidass Publishers)

But from the sixteenth century they had felt the yoke of the Mughals, Afghans, Sikhs, Dogras and, for emphasis—from their point of view—Indians, Pakistanis and Chinese. (Pakistani irregulars had invaded Jammu and Kashmir in 1948 killing, raping, and destroying, and Pakistan had forcibly occupied a third of the original area of Jammu and Kashmir. The Chinese had five thousand square miles of Aksai Chin handed over to them by the Pakistanis). But they had most resented having been sold as chattel together with the 'property' of Jammu and Kashmir by the British to the Dogras after the first Anglo-Sikh war of 1845-46.

Having lost that war—long after the death of Maharaja Ranjit Singh—the Sikhs, as indemnification for the 'expenses' of the East India Company, in addition to ceding all the 'forts, territories and rights in the Doab or country, hill and plain, situated between the rivers Beas and Sutlej' had to pay one and a half crore of rupees. Since 'the whole of this sum' was not forthcoming, there was a further cession of all* 'the forts, territories, rights and interests in the hill countries, which are situated between the rivers Beas and Indus, including the provinces of Cashmere and Hazarah'. This was by the Treaty of Lahore of 9 March 1846.

However, from Governor-General Hardinge's letters to the Secret Committee of 10 March 1846, it was evident that the Company had no intention of retaining the land between the Beas and the Indus.† 'It would bring us into collision with many powerful chiefs, for whose coercion a large military establishment at a great distance from our provinces

---

The Story of Kashmir Yesterday and Today, Vol.III, by Verinder Grover (Deep & Deep Publications), p.4

†Ibid., p.7

and military resources would be necessary. It would more than double the extent of our present frontier in countries assailable at every point, and most difficult to defend without any corresponding advantages for such large additions of territory. Now, distant and conflicting interests would be created and races of people, with whom we have hitherto had no intercourse, would be brought under our rule, while the territories, excepting Kashmir, are comparatively unproductive, and would scarcely pay the expenses of occupation and management.'

Minus 'the trans-Beas portion of Kulu and Mandi with the more fertile district and the strong position of Nurpur and the celebrated Fort Kangra the Key of the Himalayas', the territory was to be sold to Raja Gulab Singh of Jammu as a reward for his 'conduct during the late operation'. Raja Gulab Singh, one of the important generals in Maharaja Ranjit Singh's Lahore durbar, conferred by his master the rajaship of Jammu with the obligation of military duty with the Sikh Army, had on the contrary, in pursuance of an understanding with the Company—like Mir Jaffar in relation to the Battle of Plassey—kept away from the war. This was the 'conduct', for which he had had to be recompensed. The sale was at a discounted price of rupees seventy-five lakh— the Company having kept a part of the territory, now in Himachal—by the Treaty of Amritsar of 16 March 1846. Gulab Singh was again enjoined to military duty with his superiors but this time, with the East India Company.

The treatment meted out by the Dogras was no better than earlier. But the Kashmiris were no longer inert and their agitation demanding 'State for State's People' during the reign of Maharaja Pratap Singh wrung from his son, Maharaja Hari Singh, the policy of forbidding outsiders from buying immovable property in the state and the preference of 'Mulkis' (state subjects) to outsiders in government employment. Actually, this was no relief to the majority Kashmiri Muslims, as jobs were cornered by Dogras and Pandits. Exacerbating matters further, only Dogras could serve in the army or own and use firearms. But the red rag was section 298-A of the Ranbir Penal Code, by which anybody slaughtering a cow, 'wild or domesticated'—'wild' obviously a reference to nilgai, a large Indian antelope, there being no wild cattle around—could be imprisoned for ten years. (Under section 298-C the punishment for doing likewise with a he or she buffalo was just a fine five times the price of the animal.)

The oppressed Muslim majority revolted in 1931, fetched repression, but finally the maharaja's amnesty when the movement proved invincible. In response to the maharaja's call for submission of reasonable demands the Muslim memorials demanded proportionate representation in the public services, and equality of rights and treatment for all 'state subjects'. A commission—the Glancy Commission—was appointed to look into the grievances. The commission recommended religious tolerance, free studentship in due proportion to all communities, more Muslim teachers and more Muslim employment in the state services. The recommendations were accepted.

A Reform Conference under Glancy to give effect to Hari Singh's 'desire to associate his people with the administration of the State' recommended a legislative assembly which, after further work by the Franchise Committee, turned out to be a body of 75 members—15 officials and 60 non-officials, 27 of whom would be nominated and 33 elected. But the franchise was limited to lawyers, doctors, pensioned officers, title holders, village and district headmen, priests and managers of religious property, and the maharaja reserved for himself all legislative, executive and judicial powers.

Elections to the assembly, or Praja Sabha, in 1934 saw the Muslim Conference under Shiekh Abdullah, a schoolteacher, winning fourteen out of the twenty-one Muslim elected seats. But Sheikh Abdullah was not satisfied with a dummy legislature and demanded 'responsible government', to which the maharaja paid no heed. So Abdullah called for a 'Responsible Government day'. As this found little response from other communities, Abdullah changed the name of the party to National Conference. Thereafter 'Responsible Government day' garnered resolutions against irresponsible government and a united demand for responsible government.

But the maharaja still fiddled and made some sham constitutional changes in the Jammu and Kashmir Constitution Act 1939. The proof of this was the resignation of Mirza Afzal Beg—a National Conference minister in the Cabinet—because dissent from government policy was not allowed in the legislature.

Abdullah responded by rejecting Dogra sovereignty and the Treaty of Amritsar, which he called a sale deed. He also asked the maharaja to quit the Valley, bag and baggage, and let the Kashmiris decide their own future. Abdullah was put in jail and another round of repression followed.

In February 1946 it was announced that three British Cabinet ministers—hence the name Cabinet Mission—would be coming to the subcontinent to find a solution to the problem of India.

Abdullah wrote to the Cabinet Mission asking for a re-appreciation of the relationship between the Paramount Power and the maharaja of Jammu and Kashmir, because the state and its people had been sold by the British to Gulab Singh a hundred years earlier.

The Cabinet Mission ignored the Sheikh's request but generally laid down the principle that once the British withdrew from India, the rights surrendered by the states to the Paramount Power would revert to the states, and that paramountcy could not and would not be transferred to an Indian government.

As far as British India went, the colonial government in February 1947 spelled out that Muslim majority areas would constitute the Dominion of Pakistan, and Hindu majority areas the Dominion of India. For the princely states the scheme of transfer of power would be the one set out by the Cabinet Mission.

But in his address to the Chamber of Princes in July 1947, Lord Mountbatten, as crown representative, advised the princes to accede to either of the two dominions, depending on geographical contiguity, before the transfer of power on 15 August. He also warned them that if they did not link up with either they might be cut off from any source of supply.

On 15 August, Jammu and Kashmir chose to be independent, but there was soon a revolt in Poonch, which was attributed to Pakistani infiltration. Pakistan, which then controlled the only two accesses to Jammu and Kashmir, blockaded it. Hari Singh then promptly released Abdullah, as he and the National Conference were known to be opposed to Jinnah and Pakistan. When tribals and irregulars from Pakistan invaded the state on 20 October 1947 and made significant advances towards Srinagar, Hari Singh ran away to Jammu after having armed Abdullah with the office of Emergency Administrator and hoping for the best. Abdullah evidently was not so sure this was enough, and advised immediate accession to India with a view to securing military help. The maharaja acceded to India on 26 October and this must have been acutely discomfiting to Mountbatten as it violated the principles of geographical contiguity and majority population. He accepted the accession on condition that there would be a plebiscite—offering the limited choices of being either with India or Pakistan—after peace had been restored.

Pakistan rejected the accession, calling it a fraud foisted on the people of Kashmir by a pusillanimous ruler with Indian cooperation. So hostilities would continue.

Mountbatten wished to put an early end to the conflict and initially, achieving this seemed to be an in-house affair. All he had to do was to operate through the Joint Defence Council under Auchinlech and the British commanders-in-chief of the Indian and Pakistani armies. In India the Defence Committee was not even under the Council of Ministers, but Mountbatten himself. When Nehru and Vallabhbhai Patel decided on military intervention, the Defence Committee literally doodled and merely contemplated the possibility of flying in arms to Srinagar. When Nehru and Patel persisted, and insisted on airlifting a whole battalion, the Defence Committee at first dismissed it as impractical, but eventually gave in. The airlifting began on 27 October.

Pakistan then wanted to enter directly in the conflict, but Auchinlech dissuaded it on the ground that since Kashmir had acceded to India this would amount to open declaration of war against India.

Having failed to keep the Indian army out of Kashmir but succeeded in spiking Pakistan's military response, Mountbatten tried to manipulate a cessation of hostilities through a Joint Defence Council meeting in which both Nehru and Jinnah would participate. Nehru backed out, taking exception to the Pakistani comments on the accession.

So it turned out to be a battle of wits between Mountbatten and Jinnah. Jinnah seemed to be amenable to calling off the invasion, but would not accept a plebiscite with Sheikh Abdullah as prime minister of Kashmir, and the Indian army there in strength.

When hostilities had embarrassingly got out of the control of Mountbatten and his British biradari, he persuaded Nehru against his own better judgement to complain to the United Nations. The United Nations did eventually succeed in effecting a ceasefire, but only on 1 January 1949. In the meantime India agreed to a plebiscite, and the UN Security Council, in a Basic Resolution, set out two preconditions for a plebiscite—ceasefire and withdrawal from Jammu and Kashmir of the invading forces from Pakistan. Since Pakistan, at the time of the resolution, did not cease fire and subsequently never withdrew its forces from the state, the plebiscite could not come about.

The Kashmiris had had misgivings about the accession but Abdullah, who had initially seen it as a means of preventing the state from being swallowed by Pakistan and then as a portal to land reforms—acceptable to India's political regime but anathema to Pakistan's ruling feudal class—adroitly took them along with him. And they were amply rewarded, for in the breakneck land reforms the debts of the peasant were cancelled and the land was returned to him without compensation to the landlord. So in the self-same stroke the land-based economic power of the Dogras was shattered.

The land reforms were a spectacular success, but also the beginning of the Sheikh's downfall. The expropriated landlords rallied together, forming the Praja party. They were joined by the Rashtriya Swayamsevak Sangh (RSS), Jan Sangh, and Hindu Mahasabha, whose slogan was no duality of constitution, flag, and Head of State in one country—a reference to Article 370 of the Constitution of India, and the special status accorded to Jammu and Kashmir. The agitation of these reactionary forces was so vehement that the well-known Jan Sangh leader Shyama Prasad Mookerjee was to die in detention in Srinagar. In short, a standard capitalist reform measure had divided the state along communal lines—predominantly Hindu Jammu versus preponderantly Muslim Kashmir.

Besieged by communal elements, Abdullah sought an exit out of his predicament. He tested UN representative Owen Dixon with the concept of an independent Kashmir, something completely outside the frame of reference of the plebiscite offered by India and contemplated by the UN Security Council.

Not having got a signal on it, he took to chiding Nehru about communal elements that had forced Nehru's hand and prevented India from being the ideal secular state the two had once envisioned. He also fretted on matters of autonomy—gratuitous advice from Delhi on subjects unconcerned with defence, foreign affairs and communications, the only ones Jammu and Kashmir had ceded to India in the accession. At Ranbirsinghpura he castigated the attempt at fully applying the Indian Constitution to his state as 'unrealistic, childish and savouring of lunacy'.

Abdullah then met American politician and diplomat Adlai Stevenson and was thought to have canvassed Anglo-US support for Kashmiri independence. He also openly emphasized that Kashmir was neither an appendage of India nor of Pakistan. And he did all this with a touch of pique, having realized that the Government of India was already flirting with his National Conference colleague Bakshi

Ghulam Muhammad and about to drop him flat. Which it did when it finally dismissed the Sheikh and sent him to prison under the State Preventive Detention Act. The charge: conspiracy 'to overawe by force and show of force the duly constituted Government of the State of Jammu and Kashmir, with the object of overthrowing it and facilitating annexation of the State's territory by Pakistan'.*

After Sheikh Abdullah's dismissal, as though an additional irritant was necessary, Nehru made a new offer of a plebiscite, from which he tactically withdrew when Pakistan entered into a military alliance with the United States.

Reverting to Abdullah, even twenty years after his death, it is evident that one is dealing with a very complex personality. But from his experience and conduct one can try to come to some conclusions. To begin with, he was a Kashmiri nationalist. He had seen the Mulki movement, the revolt of the Muslim majority against the maharaja's regime, the Glancy Commission's recommendations in favour of redressing the imbalance in state policy against Muslims, and the creation of the Praja Sabha. He had then taken control of the agitation for responsible government and the 'Quit Kashmir' movement against the maharaja which was aborted by the abrupt end of British paramountcy and the invasion of the state by elements from Pakistan. After accession he had abolished the Dogra zamindari and had thereby effectively removed Dogra presence from the Valley.

Jammu and Kashmir could only have moved on to further social and economic development as an autonomous state. And left undisturbed, Abdullah would most certainly have become a major Indian political leader. But when

---

The Constitution of Jammu and Kashmir by Justice A.S. Anand, chapter 4, p.86

communal forces started subverting his authority and the Government of India began undermining the autonomy of the state he seemed to revert to pure Kashmiri nationalism. Here was a pragmatic politician who, when he asked the maharaja to quit Kashmir, rejected the Treaty of Amritsar and the Dogra sovereignty that derived from it. If the state could not even maintain its autonomy, was he not likely to also dismiss accession of the state to India as an expediency necessitated by the invasion of Pakistani tribals, and demand the reversion of Jammu and Kashmir to its pre-1947 situation, but with the maharaja and Dogras effectively done out of power in the meantime? How else can one understand his attempts at securing independence or self-determination for the state (when only plebiscite had been offered)?

When after eleven years in jail, Abdullah was released in 1964, he met Chou En-lai to secure China's support for Kashmir's self-determination. Back he went to confinement, and his response to the Simla Agreement at the end of the Indo-Pakistan war of 1971 was that it recognized that the future of Jammu and Kashmir had yet to be decided. Thereafter he was compromised, and after the Indira Gandhi–Sheikh Abdullah accord headed a government in a Congress-dominated assembly. He resurrected the National Conference in the 1977 elections, but died in 1982.

No other politician in power in Kashmir continued the Kashmiri nationalist tradition of Sheikh Abdullah, and if he had he would have been jailed the same way. What happened instead was the formation of a militant group in Peshawar in 1964, with the goal of an independent reunited Jammu and Kashmir, that is, Jammu and Kashmir, Pakistan-occupied Kashmir, Gilgit, Baltistan, Hunza and Aksai Chin. This was the Jammu and Kashmir National Liberation Front—JKLF, ('national' since deleted). It opened offices in the UK, France, the Netherlands, Germany, the US and four Central Asian states, before establishing a unit in Jammu and Kashmir in 1988.

The JKLF agenda was a violent one and the organization was used by Pakistan's Inter-Services Intelligence for operations in Jammu and Kashmir from 1966. But Pakistan was even less receptive than India to the idea of Kashmiri independence. They therefore organized a pro-Pakistan outfit, the Hizbul Mujahideen, to eliminate the JKLF leadership. The damage was done in the 1990s when, incidentally, Indian security forces also claimed successes against JKLF.

In 1995 a survey by *Outlook* showed 72 per cent of the people contacted in the Valley wanted an independent Jammu and Kashmir. Again, a post-2002 election survey by the Lokniti Institute for Comparative Democracy, Centre for the Study of Developing Societies, indicated that 78.8 per cent of the respondents from the Valley wanted a reunited and independent Jammu and Kashmir. Thus the goal of most of the respondents in the Valley and of JKLF coincided.

There were, however, candidates for the 1987 assembly elections representing the Muslim United Front which included Azadi groups like the Muslim Conference, the Awami Action Committee, the J&K Jamaat-e-Islami, and the Jammu and Kashmir People Conference (these groups were also in the All Peoples Hurriyat Conference, a successor to MUF). The goals of most of them were not as clearly defined as those of JKLF. An exception was the Jamaat-e-Islami, which wanted Jammu and Kashmir to join Pakistan. The MUF candidates could only contest as independents, no Azadi group being admissible for registration with the Election Commission. Parties registered with the commission have to 'uphold the sovereignty, unity and integrity of India' and to affirm their allegiance to the Constitution of India.

The 1987 elections were generally seen to have been tainted with widespread rigging, that is, booth capturing, beating and arresting polling agents, and reverse declarations of results. The most egregious example Kashmiris are fond of relating (we heard a lot of this case when we met the political parties in June 2002) was the one concerning Muhammad Yusuf—later known as Syed Salahuddin, supreme commander of the Hizbul Mujahideen. He had contested from the Ameera Kadal constituency and is said to have won but to have suffered the humiliation of seeing his National Conference opponent declared elected and the indignity of being beaten up in a police station. His polling agents were Yasin Malik (later JKLF chief in Kashmir), Javed Mir (later Yasin Malik's number two), Ashfaq Majeed and Hamid Sheikh. They all crossed to Pakistan and swore to speak with the gun.

The renamed MUF, that is, the All Party Hurriyat Conference, bolstered by the Yasin Malik faction of JKLF, understandably boycotted the 1996 elections. With all the efforts of the Americans and of the Union government through the renowned criminal lawyer-cum-politician Ram Jethmalani, the Hurriyat, except for a splinter of the Jammu and Kashmir Peoples Conference, refused to participate in the 2002 elections too.

The breakaway from JKPC (JKPC's goal was the autonomy of Jammu and Kashmir) put up two candidates who stood as independents. If there had been others from APHC, they would have done the same thing because their groups would never have affirmed their allegiance to the Indian Constitution and the Indian State. So there was no question of co-opting, as it were, any group of the Hurriyat family in the Jammu and Kashmir electoral process. What were the efforts of the Americans and the Government of India all about, then?

What was clear from all this was that the majority of people in the Valley wanted a reunited and independent Jammu and Kashmir, with JKLF—however decimated—as their main spokesman. But nobody else wanted an independent and reunited state. Not Jammu and Ladakh, not the rest of India, not Pakistan (the acronym Pakistan included Kashmir, and Pakistan's Kashmir policy was the only point of agreement for its disparate polity), not China (with so much of Aksai Chin between its teeth) and not the Americans. (After 9/11 the US would be unlikely to countenance another Muslim country in the region.)

The United States had sponsored the idea of a triangular negotiation on Jammu and Kashmir in which the people of the state were recognized as the third party. But no one expected more from it than an easing of travel and trade restrictions between Jammu and Kashmir and Pakistan-occupied Kashmir. And that too only after the state assembly elections.

{3}

Of Autonomy

Having met hurdles in the way of determining their own future, what was the Kashmiris' experience with the sovereignty and distinctiveness of the state as guaranteed by the terms of accession and by Article 370 of the Indian Constitution? (The state's scheme of autonomy as recognized by Article 370 included a separate constitution for the state.)

The relevant clauses 7 and 8 in the Instrument of Accession were—

7. Nothing in this Instrument shall be deemed to commit me in any way to acceptance of any future Constitution of India or to fetter my discretion to enter into arrangements with the Government of India under any such future Constitution.

8. Nothing in this Instrument affects the continuance of my sovereignty in and over this State, or save as provided by or under this Instrument, the exercise of any powers, authority and rights now enjoyed by me as Ruler of this State or the validity of any law at present in force in this State.

The other five hundred states had also executed such Instruments of Accession. But whereas these documents were conveniently ignored, Jammu and Kashmir's were given full value. Lord Mountbatten as governor-general had replied to the maharaja's letter (enclosing the Instrument of Accession) accepting the Instrument but stipulating that 'where the issue of accession has been the subject of dispute, the question of accession should be decided in accordance with the wishes of the people of the state' and . . . 'as soon as law and order have been restored in Kashmir and its soil cleared of the invader, the question of the State's accession should be settled by a reference to the people'. Though some of the legally-initiated opine the governor-general had no discretionary power 'to keep the question open or attach conditions to it', India chose to adhere to the commitment of a temporary accession which was to be followed by a plebiscite. In the circumstances, the arrangements for the governance of Jammu and Kashmir had to be left as undisturbed as possible.

Therefore Article 370 in the Constitution of India implicitly acknowledges some kind of an initial parity between the sovereignties of the Union and the State of Jammu and Kashmir—to be reflected in the constitutions of the two entities. Article 370 was pivotal in the context of the state's autonomy and read:

Temporary, Transitional and Special Provisions

(1) Notwithstanding anything in this Constitution—

(a) the provisions of Article 238 shall not apply in relation to the State of Jammu and Kashmir;

(b) the power of Parliament to make laws for the said State shall be limited to—

(i) those matters in the Union List and the Concurrent List which, in consultation with the Government of the State, are declared by the President to correspond to matters specified in the Instrument of Accession governing the accession of the State to the Dominion of India as the matters with respect to which the Dominion Legislature may make laws for that State; and

(ii) such other matters in the said Lists as, with the concurrence of the Government of the State, the President may by order specify.

Explanation: For the purposes of this Article, the Government of the State means the person for the time being recognised by the President as the Maharaja of Jammu and Kashmir acting on the advice of the Council of Ministers for the time being in office under the Maharaja's Proclamation dated the fifth day of March, 1948;

(c) the provisions of Article I and of this Article shall apply in relation to that State;

(d) such of the other provisions of this Constitution shall apply in relation to that State subject to such exceptions and modifications as the President may by order specify.

Provided that no such order which relates to the matters specified in the Instrument of Accession of the State referred to in paragraph (i) of sub-clause (b) shall be issued except in consultation with the Government of the State:

Provided further that no such order which relates to

matters other than those referred in the last preceding proviso shall be issued except with the concurrence of that Government.

(2) If the concurrence of the Government of the State referred to in paragraph (ii) of sub-clause (b) of clause (1) or in the second proviso to sub-clause (d) of that clause be given before the Constituent Assembly for the purpose of framing the Constitution of the State is convened, it shall be placed before such Assembly for such decision as it may take thereon.

(3) Notwithstanding anything in the foregoing provisions of this Article the President may, by public notification, declare that this Article, shall cease to be operative or shall be operative only with such exceptions and modifications and from such date as he may specify:

Provided that the recommendation of the Constituent Assembly of the State referred to in clause (2) shall be necessary before the President issues such a notification [italics mine].

Quite appropriately the Constitution (Application to Jammu and Kashmir) Order, 1950*, trod cautiously on an extremely sensitive subject. Parliament's jurisdiction was limited to defence, foreign affairs, communications—ceded to the Union by the Instrument of Accession—as well as the Union Executive and Supreme Court.

---

*The Constitution of Jammu and Kashmir by Justice A.S. Anand, chapter 4, p.109

The second part of the order looked at the relevant provisions of the Constitution of India. Part V on the Union Executive was applied to Kashmir with some modifications. The Supreme Court was accorded only appellate jurisdiction. Representatives of Jammu and Kashmir in the Council of States (also called Rajya Sabha) and the House of the People (also named Lok Sabha) not yet electable were to be appointed by the President of India in consultation with the state government. And they were allowed to vote in the election of the President.

In Part XI, dealing with relations between the Union and the states, Parliament's legislative jurisdiction was limited to the items in the Union List (matters within the exclusive legislative jurisdiction of Parliament). Since Jammu and Kashmir would be having its own constitution there would be no State List (matters within the exclusive legislative jurisdiction of the state legislature) or Concurrent List (areas where both Parliament and the state legislature could legislate). Contrary to the situation with respect to other states in the Indian Union, residuary powers of legislation were with the state legislature. Also, Parliament, in the sole exception of Jammu and Kashmir, could not dispose of any territory of the state in pursuance of an international agreement. Unlike the other states, the Union had no administrative control over Jammu and Kashmir and so could not issue directions enforcing compliance with Acts of Parliament. Specific directions on communications were therefore also barred.

Part XII, on finance, outlining the distribution of public monies from the Consolidated Funds, Public Accounts and Contingency Funds of the Union and the states and appropriations from them, was, in the case of Jammu and Kashmir, restricted to the Funds and Accounts of the Union.

Similarly the portion relating to the jurisdictions of Parliament and the state legislature on laws relating to payment, disbursement, custody and account of public monies referred only to Parliament. Taxes normally collected by the Union or state on behalf of the Union remained within the control of Jammu and Kashmir. These included income tax and customs duties.

In Part XV, on elections, the Election Commission of India's jurisdiction in relation to the state was limited to elections of the President and Vice-President of India.

Part XVI on reservations applied only to 'Scheduled Castes and Areas' in relation to parliamentary elections. Reservations to public services were restricted to Scheduled Castes in Union Services.

Part XVII on the official language confined itself to the official language of the Union which was Hindi in the Devnagri script and of the Supreme Court which was English. The state Constituent Assembly eventually decided that Urdu would be the official language of the state but that English would, unless otherwise decided by the state legislature, continue to be used for all official purposes.

Part XIX, relating to the President, governors and raj pramukhs not being liable in courts for acts done in the exercise of their official duties, was not relevant. The maharaja was protected under the Constitution Act 1939 of Jammu and Kashmir.

Part XX is about the procedure for amending the Constitution of India. Where an amendment applied to Jammu and Kashmir it would be effective only by order of the President.

Only five of the schedules to the Constitution of India were relevant to Kashmir. These related to states and their territories, emoluments of high officials, oaths of offices, representation in the Council of States and recognized official languages.

Foremost among the portions of the Constitution of India not applicable to Jammu and Kashmir was the one on Fundamental Rights. This omission was necessary because under the Kashmir land reforms no compensation was to be paid to the landlords, and this would have been repugnant to Article 31 of the Constitution. This article said no property could 'be taken possession of or required for public purposes . . . unless the law provides for compensation for the property . . .' Besides, the State Subject Act 1927, with a notification of 1932, prohibited outsiders from buying property in the state. And the invasion by Pakistan irregulars and resultant turmoil made it incumbent on the state to have its own preventive detention law.

The Directive Principles of State Policy in Part IV were not applicable as it was thought prudent to leave this to the consideration of the state Constituent Assembly which was drafting its own constitution.

Part XIV dealing with services did not apply. The state services were governed by the Kashmir Civil Services Regulation under which only 'permanent residents' of the state could be employed.

Part XVIII is about a variety of proclamations of Emergency; Article 352 for general emergency, Article 356 for failure of the constitutional machinery of the state; Article 360 for financial emergency. Out of these, only Article 352 was extended to Jammu and Kashmir with the difference that the President on his own could not issue a proclamation if there was a general emergency arising from internal disturbance. But if the state government felt the internal disturbance was compelling it could request the President for a proclamation.

If anything the Constitution (Application to Jammu and Kashmir) Order 1950 positively restricted the sovereignty of the Union in Jammu and Kashmir and emphasized the areas where the Constitution of India would not apply. It all changed with the Constitution (Application to Jammu and Kashmir) Order 1954 and subsequent orders of a similar kind. The sovereignty of Jammu and Kashmir was suddenly deluged by the Union's through the twin sluices of Article 370, that is, Parliament's legislative jurisdiction and the application of existing provisions of the Constitution.

Article 246 of the Constitution is the one laying down the separate and concurrent legislative jurisdictions of Parliament and state legislatures. With respect to Jammu and Kashmir, Parliament's province was stretched from the original defence, foreign affairs and communications to all matters within the Union List. Of course, there were notable exceptions, such as:

- the Central Bureau of Intelligence and Investigation;
- legislation on preventive detention for reasons connected with Defence, Foreign Affairs and Security of India. (However, under the Foreigners Act, 1946, the Union Government could intern or expel foreigners where required);
- acquisition or requisition of property;
- court of wards for the estates of rulers of Indian states;
- censorship of cinematographic films;
- ancient and historical monuments, archaeological sites and remains;
- interstate migration or quarantine (to safeguard the privileges of 'permanent residents' within the state);

- the constitution, organization and jurisdiction of the Jammu and Kashmir High Court (the appointment of judges under the Jammu and Kashmir Constitution was by the President in consultation with the Chief Justice of India and the state governor. The transfer of judges in relation to the Jammu and Kashmir High Court was enabled by clause (1A) of Article 222 of the Constitution of India);

- elections to the state legislature (these elections were to be conducted according to the provisions of the Jammu and Kashmir Representation of People Act. Nevertheless, the jurisdiction of the Election Commission of India was extended to the state by an amendment in 1959 to the Jammu and Kashmir Constitution);

- the audit of the accounts of the state. (But two years later the jurisdiction of the Comptroller and Auditor General included the state.)

The Concurrent List was originally not applicable to Jammu and Kashmir since anything outside the Union List was within the residuary legislative jurisdiction of the state legislature. Some of the unchanged items and a few changed items—the rest deleted—of this list were also made applicable after amendments to the Constitution of India. But at least Article 370 mentions matters in the Union List and Concurrent List as within the competence of Parliament in relation to Jammu and Kashmir.

Even though residuary legislation was with the state legislature Article 248 was made to apply to the state to enable Parliament to legislate to prevent terrorist activities. It referred to—

Prevention of activities—

(a) involving terrorist acts directed towards overawing the Government as by law established or striking terror in the people or any section of the people or alienating any section of the people or adversely affecting the harmony amongst different sections of the people;

(b) *directed towards disclaiming, questioning or disrupting the sovereignty and territorial integrity of India or bringing about cession of a part of the territory of India or secession of a part of territory of India from the Union or causing insult to the Indian National Flag, the Indian National Anthem and this Constitution* [italics mine].

The Union's sovereignty had encroached on the state's sovereignty also by way of executive directions, the primacy of the Supreme Court within the judicial system, emergency powers, financial powers and the enforcement of fundamental rights.

By Articles 256 and 257 the Union directions to the state cover compliance with Union and existing laws and exercising the executive power of the state in a way which does not interfere with the executive power of the Union, protection of railways and construction and maintenance of means of communication of military importance. Both articles were applied to Jammu and Kashmir. In addition a proviso was added to Article 256 which enjoined the state to exercise its executive power in facilitating the Union in the discharge of its constitutional duties and responsibilities with respect to Jammu and Kashmir. This particularly applied to acquiring or requisitioning property for the Union or transferring state property to the Union. However

Article 365, which deals with a presidential proclamation in consequence of a state's not complying with the directions of Article 256 and 257, was withheld from Jammu and Kashmir.

Article 261 is about faith and credit to public acts, records and judicial proceedings throughout India which says that the manner and conditions under which they shall be proved will be laid down by law made by Parliament. While Article 261 was extended to Kashmir, the proof would be by law laid down by the state legislature as well.

Article 263 empowers the President to set up an inter-state council on inter-state disputes, identifying common interests and recommendations 'for the better coordination of policy and action'. The article was made to apply to Jammu and Kashmir without any changes. The state became a member of the North Zonal Council.

The Supreme Court in India is at the apex of a unitary judicial system. Article 141 says that the law laid down by the Supreme Court is binding on all Indian courts. Article 144 requires all authorities civil and judicial to act in aid of the Supreme Court. Article 131 is on the original jurisdiction of the Supreme Court, that is, in deciding disputes between the Government of India and one or more states or between the Government of India and one or more states on one side and one or more states on the other side, or between two or more states. Article 133 refers to the Supreme Court's appellate jurisdiction. Article 136 is about the court's jurisdiction on special leave to appeal. Article 143 refers to the Supreme Court's advisory role on presidential references. Article 139 refers to the Court's writ jurisdiction. All these were applied to Jammu and Kashmir, but there were some modifications. In criminal matters relating to the appellate jurisdiction of the Court, Parliament could in the rest of

India by law confer more powers on the Supreme Court. Where Jammu and Kashmir was concerned Parliament could do so only on the request of the state legislature. Secondly, the state high court, which under the state constitution had no writ jurisdiction in relation to authorities outside the state, was given powers to issue writs to them under Article 226 of the Constitution of India.

Among the Emergency Provisions, Article 356 relating to a breakdown of the constitutional machinery in the state was made to apply to Jammu and Kashmir with the difference that the Constitution referred to was not to be only the Constitution of India but also the state constitution. In addition, the Constitution of Jammu and Kashmir's Section 92 provided for governor's rule in case of failure of the constitutional machinery in the state. Article 356 and Section 92 were intended to co-exist and supplement each other. And governor's rule being only for six months had to be converted to President's rule if the failure of the constitutional machinery continued beyond that period.

Article 13 of the Indian Constitution declares that all laws inconsistent with Fundamental Rights shall to the extent of the inconsistency be void. Article 13 in reference to Jammu and Kashmir was modified so that its application was not from the commencement of the Indian Constitution but from the Constitution (Application to Jammu and Kashmir) Order, 1954. This was necessary to protect the state government's legislation which returned the land to the peasant without compensation to the landlords.

Article 14 guarantees equality before the law or equal protection of the laws. It was applied to Kashmir. However, the Supreme Court found nothing wrong with the Jammu and Kashmir Enemy Agents Ordinance which has a procedure for the trial of an 'enemy' and an 'enemy agent' different from the one provided in Criminal Procedure. The court considered the ordinance was based on a reasonable classification considering the circumstances in the state.

Article 15, which prohibits discrimination exclusively on religion, race, caste, sex, place of birth, applied to Jammu and Kashmir.

Article 16, on equality of opportunity in matters of public employment, also applied. But the clause enabling Parliament to make a law prescribing 'in regard to a class or classes of employment, or appointment to an office under the government of, or any local or other authority within, a state or Union territory, any requirement as to residence within that state or Union territory prior to such appointment' was deleted. This was to avoid conflict with the state legislature which had the power to define classes of persons qualifying as permanent residents with special rights and privileges.

Article 19 protects the freedom of speech and expression, of assembly, of association, of movement, of residence in settlement, of property and of profession, occupation, trade or business. But barring the first and the last freedoms Parliament can impose reasonable restrictions. With Jammu and Kashmir there were modifications for a period of ten years with effect from 14 May 1954. The freedoms of assembly, association, movement, residence and property were subjected to restrictions relating to the security of the state. And these 'reasonable restrictions' were not subject to judicial review.

Article 21 says no person shall be deprived of his life or personal liberty except according to the procedure established by law. Which means that procedure has to be 'laid down by a competent Legislature'. The article was extended to Jammu and Kashmir.

Article 22 is about safeguards against arbitrary detention in connection with the security of a state or the maintenance of public order or the maintenance of supplies and services essential to the community or defence, foreign affairs or the security of India. The detention can ordinarily be only for three months. Parliament can legislate providing for classes of cases in which detention can exceed three months but only with the prior approval of an advisory board. And the detaining authority is required to communicate at the earliest to the detenu the grounds of detention and give him an opportunity to represent against the order of detention. Article 22 also applied to Jammu and Kashmir except that the power of legislation on the subject was with the state legislature and not with Parliament.

Articles 25 to 30 which guarantee religious and cultural rights were extended without modification.

The right to property was dealt with in articles 19 and 31 of the Constitution, as originally enacted and both were subject to 'reasonableness of restrictions'. Article 31(1) said no one could be deprived of his property save with the authority of law, that is, by legislation. Article 31(2) allowed acquisition or requisition of property only for public purposes, and that too under the authority of law which had to provide for compensation and either fixed the amount of compensation or specified the principles for determining the compensation. Article 31(3) said that any expropriatory law had to have the assent of the President. Article 31(4) protected laws reifying from bills pending in the state legislatures at the commencement of the Constitution of India. Article 31(5) said:

Nothing in clause (2) shall affect—
(a) the provisions of any existing law other than a law to which the provisions of clause (6) apply, or

(b) the provisions of any law which the State may hereafter make—
(i) for the purpose of imposing or levying any tax or penalty, or
(ii) for the promotion of public health or the prevention of danger to life or property, or
(iii) *in pursuance of any agreement entered into between the Government of the Dominion of India or the Government of India and the Government of any other country, or otherwise, with respect to property declared by law to be evacuee property* [italics mine].

And Article 31(6) protected a state law enacted not more than eighteen months before the commencement of the Constitution of India which was duly certified by the President.

In relation to Jammu and Kashmir clauses 3, 4 and 6 were omitted. And clause 5 was substituted by another which read:

Nothing in clause (2) shall effect:
(a) the provisions of any existing law; or
the provisions of any law which the State may hereafter make.
(i) for purposes of imposing or levying any penalty; or
(ii) for the promotion of public health or the prevention of danger to life and property; or
(iii) with respect to property declared by law to be evacuee property.

The substitution was to protect the state land reforms and this was formally recognized by the Supreme Court in a case which went up to it.

Under Article 32, the Supreme Court had been given the power to enforce fundamental rights through a variety of writs. This was applicable to the state. However, since the power to issue writs under Article 226 was earlier withheld from the Jammu and Kashmir High Court, this power was conferred on it by clause 2(A), though only in relation to writs for the enforcement of Fundamental Rights. And of course clause 3 of Article 32 which authorized Parliament by law to empower any other court to exercise within its jurisdiction all or any of the powers of the Supreme Court was not extended to Jammu and Kashmir.

Under Article 33 Parliament can determine to what extent Fundamental Rights should apply to armed forces or forces charged with the maintenance of public order. And Article 34 enables Parliament to indemnify anyone in the service of the Union or of the state or any other person in respect of any act in connection with maintenance or restoration of order where martial law was in force. Both were applied to Jammu and Kashmir.

In addition, a flood of Central Acts was made applicable to the state, including old familiars like the Negotiable Instruments Act, Police Act, Post Office Act, Explosive Substances Act, Workmen's Compensation Act, Trade Union Act, Payment of Wages Act, Arbitration Act, Insurance Act, Motor Vehicles Act, Central Excise and Sales Tax Act, Industrial Disputes Act, Minimum Wages Act, Census Act, Representation of the People Acts, 1950 and 1951, All India Services Act, Mines Act, Commissions of Enquiry Act, Excise Duty Act, Prevention of Food Adulteration Act, Companies Act, Suppression of Immoral Traffic in Women and Girls Act, Wealth Tax Act, Arms Act, Income Tax Act, Delimitation Act, 1972, Foreign Exchange Regulation Act, Essential Services Maintenance Act, etc., etc.

The sovereignty of Jammu and Kashmir had been compromised also by amendments/enactments in the state constitution. The Sadar-i-Riyasat was required to be a permanent resident of the state and he was elected by the state assembly. He was not only an insider but could be removed only by impeachment. The constitutional amendment reduced him to a mere governor holding office at the pleasure of the President and he could be from anywhere else in India. Similarly the Prime Minister of Kashmir, or Wazir-i-Azam, was by the same method downgraded to ordinary chief minister. Again, Section 138 of the state constitution was amended to entrust the Election Commission of India with the superintendence, direction and control of the preparation of electoral rolls and conduct of elections to either House of the state legislature.

But the most crucial was Section 92* of the state constitution, which allowed the Sadar-i-Riyasat—substituted by governor—to proclaim governor's rule in case of failure of the constitutional (in terms of the Jammu and Kashmir constitution) machinery in the state, only with the concurrence of the President.

How much of the state's sovereignty remained? Unlike any other state Jammu and Kashmir had its own flag (rectangular, red, with three equidistant white, vertical stripes and a white plough in the middle) and its own official language (Urdu, but English would continue to be used for all official purposes as before the commencement of the state constitution).

The governor and high court judges were appointed under the state constitution. And this constitution could be amended only by the introduction of a bill which was

---

*The Constitution of Jammu and Kashmir, 1957

required to be passed in each House by a majority of not less than two-thirds of the total membership of that House before the assent of the governor.

Residuary legislation, apart from the modifications in item 97 of the Union List, and Article 248 of the Indian Constitution allowing Parliament to legislate on prevention of activities involving terrorist acts, had been left with the state legislature. So civil and criminal law, normal preventive detention and acquisition and requisition of property which are in the Concurrent List fell in the state legislature's domain. The state continued using the Ranbir Penal Code, Jammu and Kashmir Criminal Procedure Code and the Civil Procedure Code, the Jammu and Kashmir Preventive Detention Act and the Big Landed Estates Abolition Act, 1950 and the Jammu and Kashmir Agrarian Reforms Act, 1978. Though the Courts of Wards for the estates of rulers of Indian states, regulation of mines and mineral development in the public interest, and elections to the legislatures of states are in the Union List, the Union chose to keep these matters in the province of the state and elections to the assembly were conducted according to the provisions of the state constitution, the Jammu and Kashmir Representation of the People Act, 1957, the J&K Registration of Electors Rules, 1966 and the Jammu and Kashmir Conduct of Elections Rules, 1965.

Mention has been made that only permanent residents of the state were allowed to vote and stand for assembly elections. There were other eccentricities in the state's electoral dispensation. Section 24-F of the J&K Representation of the People Act said that if a civil or criminal court, tribunal or board or commission set up under a statute found anyone to have illegally or by corrupt means or by otherwise abusing or misusing the position held by him as member of either House of the state legislature, or of Parliament or any office held by him by virtue of being such member obtained for himself or for any of his relatives any valuable things or pecuniary advantage, he might be disqualified from standing for elections to the state legislature for a period of ten years. The delimitation of assembly constituencies was done according to the provisions of the Jammu and Kashmir Constitution and the Jammu and Kashmir Representation of the People Act. And a separate Delimitation Commission was contemplated, though in practice the Central Delimitation Commission also functioned as State Delimitation Commission in 1963 and 1973. Since no Central Delimitation Commission was set up in the 1980s, the state, after the 1981 census, constituted a three-member commission. So Jammu and Kashmir was the only state with its own Delimitation Commission. It is another matter that the commission of two judges and a deputy election commissioner of the Election Commission of India could complete delimitation on the 1981 census only in 1995.

It needs to be mentioned that since the Indira Gandhi government's proclamation of an emergency, the Jammu and Kashmir Assembly had been the only legislature not to have reverted to the original duration of five years. To that extent it had been giving itself an extra year in every term.

I have referred to the orthodox Hindu elements' objection to two constitutions, flags and heads of state, essentially symbols of the arrangement under Article 370 of the Indian Constitution. Of real substance was the perception that the communal disturbances since 1986 and exodus of 300,000 Pandits beginning in 1990 had been part of deliberate religious cleansing by the preponderant Muslim majority in the Valley. All too reminiscent of the events of Partition. Besides, it was felt that Hindu-majority Jammu and Buddhist-majority Ladakh were not only neglected by the state government but were very happy to be with India. The solution, therefore, was to allow people from other parts of India to settle in Jammu and Kashmir so as to tilt the balance against the Muslim majority. However, the state laws allowed only permanent residents of the state to settle within it, and this was protected by the Indian Constitution.

Again it was the same 'permanent residents' only who could man the state's services and be elected as MLAs. This imparted an impression of inbreeding in the governance of the state.

Depending on the matters extended to the state, the Union had no trouble getting the required concurrence or approval of the state government, or the approval of the state assembly. This also applied to amending the Jammu and Kashmir constitution to demote the Sadar-i-Riyasat and Wazir-e-Azam to governor and chief minister respectively and allow the jurisdiction of the Election Commission of India into the state. There was also a specific provision for governor's rule in the context of failure of the constitutional machinery in the state. Were the politicians in power in Delhi and Srinagar in fact working in tandem for the early integration of the state within the Union?

It is well to recall Sheikh Abdullah's vociferous opposition to the state's loss of autonomy since 1953. His son Farooq had later rued the same development in the run up to the 1996 elections and even appointed a committee on internal autonomy, chaired by former Sadar-i-Riyasat Dr Karan Singh, to recommend measures for the unwinding of the Union's bonds on the state and the restoration of autonomy to it, going back to the Instrument of Accession, the Constitution (Application to Jammu and Kashmir) Order of 1950 and the Delhi Agreement of 1952. But you don't turn a decisive course of history with committee recommendations.

4

Of Manipulative Politics

Kashmiris' being able to decide on their future was evidently snarled beyond undoing and the struggle to retain autonomy irrevocably lost. Could they at least have a government of their choice?

What did the past record indicate? Before the niceties of election they found themselves a natural leader in Sheikh Abdullah who led the quit Kashmir movement against the maharaja and then as prime minister dismantled the state's feudal structure. His counterpart in Delhi was Nehru. It was seen as fortunate that there was a symbiotic relationship between them. Nehru forced the maharaja to release the agitating Sheikh Abdullah and left no doubt in anybody's mind that the accession was on condition that Abdullah would be in control of the affairs of Jammu and Kashmir. For it was only he who could mobilize popular support behind a rather thin Indian army that was desperately trying to expel the invader. On the other hand, Abdullah needed Nehru's tacit approval for Kashmiri land reforms (though governments in states under Congress rule were eventually rather less effective in implementing land reforms). But there was an underlying contradiction between them. Nehru was for integrating the state with India. This, however, was so intolerable to the Sheikh in the context of a growing communal agitation against him, that he mooted the idea of an independent Jammu and Kashmir, even though, as he had pointed out, the state would probably never be allowed to remain independent since in the short time that it was, it was invaded by elements from Pakistan. So Abdullah's dismissal from the post of prime minister of the state and his arrest and detention in 1953 were inevitable. From the Kashmiris' point of view, however, this development was a tragedy brought about by communal elements in Indian politics.

Bakshi Ghulam Muhammad replaced him as prime minister and having served Delhi's interest but beginning to be difficult, he was made to resign under the guise of the Kamaraj Plan in which Congress politicians in power, no longer wanted by Delhi, were made to 'voluntarily' abdicate. Within a year Bakshi had been arrested under the Defence of India Rules and put in jail.

Exit Bakshi Ghulam Muhammad, enter Shams-ud-Din. After the Holy Relic incident in the Hazratbal Shrine, exit Shams-ud-Din, enter G.M. Sadiq. Since Nehru had barred the Congress from Jammu and Kashmir it could only enter the state covertly as a cuckoo laying its egg in the nest of what was then only nominally the National Conference. (Abdullah had taken the real National Conference with him to jail, later calling it the Plebiscite Front—in jest to match Nehru's offer of a plebiscite after Abdullah was in the klinks?) But once Nehru died, Bakshi and Sadiq found their true colours in the Congress and announced its entry into the state. The cuckoo had not only hatched but was to swallow its host altogether at the merger of the Congress and National Conference six months later.

The 1967 assembly elections were the first outing for the Congress, and with Sheikh Abdullah interned in south India, it secured as many as sixty-one seats. The Congress had surely found its roots. Towards the end of an eventful term which saw the launching of the first significant Pakistani-sponsored terrorist outfit, Al Fateh, the hijacking of an Indian Airlines aircraft by Kashmiri Muslim terrorists and the beginning of a full-scale offensive along the Jammu and Kashmir border by Pakistan, G.M. Sadiq passed away and Mir Qasim took over as chief minister.

Then came the 1972 assembly elections and with no competition, the Congress took fifty-eight seats. But a triumphant and generous Indira Gandhi made an accord with a relenting Abdullah who, after Pakistan had been shattered and dismembered in the 1971 war with India, no longer saw the possibility of credibly using Pakistan against India in the interest of Jammu and Kashmir. He was even persuaded to head a four-member Cabinet of independents with Congress support only to experience the underpinnings to his outfit being suddenly removed at a later stage. By then—March 1977—the Jammu and Kashmir political creatures of the Congress government in Delhi had drafted the constitution of Jammu and Kashmir, particularly Section 92, which provided for governor's rule in case of failure of the constitutional machinery in the state. Though the Congress was in the majority and could have formed their own government, they chose not to, and governor's rule followed.

In response to being convicted of electoral corruption, Indira Gandhi had declared an emergency but lost the parliamentary elections of 1977. For his part the Sheikh won the assembly elections, the National Conference having revived, and the Janata Party, then heading the government in Delhi, having taken second position in the state. This is the election the Kashmiris had later held up as a model election. The year 1977 was a high-water mark in the political relations between Delhi and Srinagar and the prime minister, Morarji Desai, was given credit for it.

By the time of the assembly elections in 1983 Indira Gandhi was back in power. But Farooq Abdullah had replaced his father Sheikh Abdullah, who had died in 1982. In the 1983 assembly elections the National Conference got a majority. However, the Congress had recouped and secured twenty-six seats. Farooq ought to have enjoyed a full term as chief minister but in the event was dismissed after one year. He had been hobnobbing with the opposition parties and Indira Gandhi had engineered the necessary defections in his party, as well as in his family. A reflection of the absurdity of the situation was Farooq's succession as chief minister by his brother-in-law G.M. Shah, who then headed a split group of the National Conference named after Khalida, Shah's wife and Farooq's sister. This was perhaps the nadir in the relations between Delhi and Srinagar.

Shah was dismissed in the midst of widespread communal disturbances in the Valley and governor's rule came in handy once again. Governor's rule having run its course of six months, President's rule was imposed for the first time (Article 356 had been extended to Jammu and Kashmir as early as December 1964). But President's rule was only meant to be a breather for the Congress—which had split the National Conference—to manoeuvre itself back into power in the company of one part of the National Conference or the other. In the context of the Rajiv Gandhi–Farooq Abdullah accord it chose the main arm of the National Conference, putting together a coalition government for just over four months before the next assembly elections. In the

1987 elections, the National Conference, the party of the Valley, and the Congress, the outsider, fought the election together and were perceived to have cheated the Muslim United Front of several seats in Kashmir. Unwittingly, perhaps, Rajiv Gandhi, who had taken the initiative for the coalition with the National Conference, had thrust the state into full-scale militancy.

Farooq ought to have continued as chief minister till 1993 but because of differences with the Government of India over the release of militants in exchange for the Union home minister's abducted daughter he resigned after a little over two and half years. Since the Congress was no longer in power in Delhi the old option of finding another chief minister from the ranks of the National Conference was no longer available. By January 1990 governor's rule had been imposed. This was followed by President's rule in July. There were six-and-half years—more than one assembly term—of non-representative government.

The National Conference won the 1996 assembly elections and, with the Congress in the wilderness in Delhi and Farooq later taking a political insurance policy by joining the BJP-led National Democratic Alliance, he was sure to enjoy his full tenure as chief minister. But would Farooq and the BJP—which ruled in Delhi—re-enact 1987?

5

EC's Constitutional Status

From what has gone before the Government of India was evidently not viewed in the best light in Kashmir. But how was it that the Election Commission of India, one of the most respected institutions in the land, was still seen out there as an appendage of the Union Executive? In answering this seeming contradiction one is drawn into abstruse institutional history. What is to be noted is that the Election Commission has been rather long in asserting itself, especially in Jammu and Kashmir.

Article 324 of the Constitution of India says:

(1) The superintendence, direction and control of the preparation of the electoral rolls for, and the conduct of, all elections to Parliament and to the Legislature of every State and of elections to the offices of President and Vice-President held under this Constitution shall be vested in a Commission (referred to in this Constitution as the Election Commission).

(2) The Election Commission shall consist of the Chief Election Commissioner and such number of other Election Commissioners, if any, as the President may from time to time fix and the appointment of

the Chief Election Commissioner and other Election Commissioners shall, subject to the provisions of any law made in that behalf by Parliament, be made by the President.

(3) When any other Election Commissioner is so appointed the Chief Election Commissioner shall act as the Chairman of the Election Commission.

(4) Before each general election to the House of the People and to the Legislative Assembly of each State, and before the first general election and thereafter before each biennial election to the Legislative Council of each State having such Council, the President may also appoint after consultation with the Election Commission such Regional Commissioners as he may consider necessary to assist the Election Commission in the performance of the functions conferred on the Commission by clause (1).

(5) Subject to the provisions of any law made by Parliament, the conditions of service and tenure of office of the Election Commissioners and the Regional Commissioners shall be such as the President may by rule determine:

Provided that the Chief Election Commissioner shall not be removed from his office except in like manner and on the like grounds as a judge of the Supreme Court and the conditions of service of the Chief Election Commissioner shall not be varied to his disadvantage after his appointment:

Provided further that any other Election Commissioner or a Regional Commissioner shall not be removed from office except on the recommendation of the Chief Election Commissioner.

(6) The President, or the Governor of a State, shall, when so requested by the Election Commission, make available to the Election Commission or to a Regional Commissioner such staff as may be necessary for the discharge of the functions conferred on the Election Commission by clause (1).

To summarize, it deals with the functions—superintendence, direction and control of the preparation of electoral rolls (including their periodic revision) and conduct of elections—and scope—elections to Parliament, the state legislatures and the offices of President and Vice-President—of the Election Commission of India. It is also about the permanent and temporary functionaries of the commission, their conditions of service and tenure, as well as the obligation of the Union and state governments to make available to the commission the staff necessary for it to discharge its duties.

The debate in the Constituent Assembly of 15 June 1949, on the proposed Article 289 (present Article 324) discloses an almost pathological obsession with clean elections. So much so that 'the independence of the elections and the avoidance of any interference by the Executive' were initially sought to be incorporated as a Fundamental Right under the Chapter on Fundamental Rights.

It was not that elections were unknown in British India. The Indian Councils Act 1909, part of the Minto-Morley Reforms, provided elections to the legislative councils under the governor-general and provincial governors. But these elections were based on the limited suffrage of special constituencies, namely municipalities, district and local boards, universities, chambers of commerce, trade associations, landholders, tea planters and others. Elections were also part of the Government of India Act, 1919, under the umbrella of the Montagu-Chelmsford Reforms. Elections were to be even more important under the Government of India Act, 1935, envisaging a more complex bicameral federal legislature, but this part never came about. All these elections were simple affairs involving small numbers, and were conducted by the authorities at the Centre and the states.

With universal adult suffrage for Parliament and the state legislatures visualized by the Constituent Assembly for independent India, conducting elections could no longer be left in the hands of amateurs, especially when they were also functionaries of Union or state governments that could no longer be trusted to be impartial. But there was a long debate on whether there should be one Central Election Commission, or one for the Centre and one each for the states. At the cost of some acrimony on the alleged attempt by some to overcentralize arrangements, it was decided that there would be just one Election Commission for the whole country.

Was the Election Commission to be a permanent or ad hoc body? Elections came after every five years and the temptation was to think that the Election Commission was in carnival every time the elections were around and sat contemplating its navel in between. But there were going to be bye-elections and assemblies dissolved before time, so some election or the other would be occupying the commission during the year. It had to be a permanent fixture with somebody always there in charge. That would be the chief election commissioner. Dr Ambedkar's scheme, however, visualized an adaptable approach, election commissioners at headquarters and regional election commissioners in the field being appointed when general elections hove in sight. There was to be no separate staff in the field, the object being to save on cost and duplication of functionaries. At election time the Government of India and state governments would provide the necessary complement of staff.

Since the primary purpose was to insulate the Election Commission from the political Executive it was insisted that the chief election commissioner should not be removed from office 'except in like manner and on the like grounds as a judge of the Supreme Court'. In other words, he could be removed only by impeachment on a resolution passed by a two-thirds majority of the members present in both Houses of Parliament. Also his conditions of service 'shall not be varied to his disadvantage after his appointment'. No qualifications were laid down for the chief election commissioner and the service conditions and tenure would be subject to the provisions of any law passed by Parliament. He was to be appointed by the President.

In keeping with the Election Commission's distance from the political Executive, it was strongly urged by some members that the appointment of the chief election commissioner should be ratified by a two-thirds majority of each of the two Houses of Parliament. But this was given a pass. (From one's own experience, mass approval by politicians of whatever persuasion or shade tends to get limited to a few self-serving people, so the pre-ratification arrangement with which many Americans are familiar but not necessarily too satisfied about, is often not the best one in practice).

A better suggestion from the Goswami Committee on electoral reforms was that the chief election commissioner should be appointed by the President in consultation with the Chief Justice of India and leader of the opposition in the House of the People (the Lok Sabha). This was followed by a bill, the Constitution (70th Amendment) Bill, 1990, introduced in the Council of States and providing for the appointment of the chief election commissioner by the President in consultation with the chairman of the Council of States, the Speaker of the Lok Sabha and the leader of the opposition in the Lok Sabha. The effort came to naught as the bill had to be withdrawn.

The President had been appointing the CEC on the recommendation of the prime minister after consulting his Council of Ministers. A crucial functionary who had to be absolutely even-handed between the parties in power and their opponents at the elections had to be cleared only by the party/parties in control of the Union government. To that extent the system of appointment had been one-sided. Yet most of the CECs had been remarkably even-handed.

Not stipulating qualifications had not been damaging to the institution, for the functions of the chief election commissioner, though often quasi-judicial, were mostly executive–managerial, and the post had always been filled by a retired secretary general of the Lok Sabha or secretary/ Cabinet secretary of the Union Government.

What had belittled the institution was leaving the tenure and terms and conditions of service to the future. The Government of India sat on the matter for twenty-two years before spelling out the status, pay and tenure of the CEC— in the Chief Election Commissioner (Conditions of Service) Rules, 1972. This was a slipshod effort as rules of this kind were normally made on the basis of specific Acts of Parliament. There was no Act then, so the rules were based on Article 324 of the Constitution itself. Even worse, after two decades a lower status for the chief election commissioner was midwived into the world in a sly manner—the rules not having to be discussed in Parliament as an Act would have had to be. The pay and emoluments were those of a mere secretary to the Government of India and the tenure, five years. The Constitution had already provided that the chief election commissioner, like a judge of the Supreme Court, could be removed only by impeachment. Obviously the status contemplated was that of a judge of the Supreme Court. In which case he could also have worked till he was sixty-five. In fairness one must admit, however, that each of the first two chief election commissioners enjoyed an unusually long innings (eight to nine years).

Even the necessary legislation, by way of the Chief Election Commissioner and other Election Commissioners (Conditions of Service) Act, 1991, was involuntary. It was in response to observations of the Supreme Court on an appeal by S.S. Dhanoa against a presidential order which reverted the Election Commission to a single-member body, Dhanoa and V.S. Seigell having been earlier appointed as election commissioners by the President in October 1989. Originally, the status of the chief election commissioner was to be raised to the Cabinet secretary's and V.S. Rama Devi, secretary to the Government of India, Legislative Department, already officiating as chief election commissioner—Peri-Sastri, the previous chief election commissioner, having died in office—was to be appointed to the post. However, in the political flux of turnstile prime ministerial tenures, Chandra Shekhar's government chose to go out of its way to induct Tirunellai Narayanaiyer Seshan as chief election commissioner. It was only then that the chief election commissioner was able to enjoy the same salary and perquisites as of a judge of the Supreme Court and to retire at the same age: sixty-five years. Of course if his tenure, then increased to six years, was over before he was sixty-five, he would retire earlier. There was another amendment in 1993 which left the chief election commissioner where he was but raised his colleagues to the same level.

The initially obscure status of the Election Commission was a blight on the institution. The Election Commission was brought up in the humble Second World War barracks on Aurangzeb Road from which it later slunk to another set of barracks, considered more respectable for their propinquity to Parliament House. In 1969 the then chief election commissioner, S.P. Sen-Varma, the first to wake up to the realization that the commission was a constitutional body like the Supreme Court, the Comptroller and Auditor General and the Union Public Service Commission, and like them should have its own building, wrote to that effect to the Government of India. Sen-Varma—considering the long mileage in time and correspondence that usually goes with the fulfilment of such requests—had the windfall of laying the foundation stone for Nirvachan Sadan on Ashok Road just one year afterwards. And the building too came up after only two years. But it was not exclusively for the Election Commission—the Border Security Force, Insurance Division of the Ministry of Finance, Central Secretariat Section and Pensioners and Grievances Cell, Department of Personnel and Controller of Accounts, and the Ministry of Law, Justice and Company Affairs shared floors with it. It was left to Seshan to take the sumptuous pleasure of evicting all of them.

6

. . . And Financial

Financially the Election Commission was in abject submission to the Ministry of Law. The chief election commissioner was just head of department under the Delegation of Financial Powers Rules, 1958 and had to supplicate the ministry for hosting a working lunch or dinner for participants in a conference even when they were electoral functionaries like chief electoral officers and district election officers.

There was a slight improvement in December 1967. The chief election commissioner was still designated as head of department but enjoyed the enhanced powers of the Ministry of Law which were re-delegated to him. However, there was still a catch or two. Copies of sanctions and other relevant orders still had to be sent to the ministry. Budget estimates and revised estimates were incorporated by the ministry in its own proposals after imposing cuts and modifications. Even interest-free and other advances applicable to commission employees in the same way as to government servants could be made only after confirmation—with the ministry—of the availability of funds. Where the ban on the creation of posts had been specially waived for it the Election Commission was still required to approach the finance ministry for posts, even at deputy secretary level.

The Election Commission's financial equation with the Government of India underwent a violent, qualitative change in July 1992 when Seshan unilaterally repudiated his status as head of department. He grandiloquently told the ministries of law and finance that the commission had decided to have its own financial arrangement as operating the funds with the concurrence of the financial adviser of the Ministry of Law was beneath the status of the commission as a constitutional body. As though as an afterthought, the Ministry of Law was asked to ensure the vacation by 31 August 1992 of the space occupied in Nirvachan Sadan by the Principal Accounts Office and Pay and Accounts Office working under the administrative control of that ministry.

The finance ministry, in July 1992 itself, meekly deleted the entry showing the chief election commissioner as head of department in the Delegation of Financial Rules, 1958. While the law ministry was yet weighing the idea of a financial adviser as consultant to the chief election commissioner, the commission promulgated 'The Election Commission of India Financial Procedures Order, 1992' on the basis of minutes of a meeting in the office of the additional secretary, budget (Ministry of Finance) on 18 September 1992. The salient features of the order were:

01. The Election Commission will have its own financial procedure, not repugnant to the accounting rules, codes and manuals issued by the President on the advice of the Comptroller and Auditor-General under Article 150 of the Constitution and statutory rules issued by the Finance Ministry under Article 283 of the Constitution which are binding on all

authorities dealing with the Consolidated Fund and public account of the Government of India.

02. An officer working in the Election Commission will be designated as the Internal Financial Advisor of the Commission to assist the Chief Election Commissioner in the discharge of the Commission's financial powers, without reference to the Ministry of Law and Justice within the powers equivalent to a Ministry.

03. The Commission will have an independent Pay and Accounts Office with staff taken on deputation wherever special skills are required.

04. No unilateral changes will be made by the Ministry of Law in the Budget grant of the Election Commission or Budget Estimates proposed by the Commission. Changes, if any, will be made after discussion and agreement between the Chief Election Commissioner's representative, Additional Secretary (Budget) and Additional Secretary and Financial Advisor (Law). The budget provisions in respect of the Election Commission will continue to be included in the Demands for Grants of the Ministry.

05. Within the budget allotted to the Election Commission as per the Appropriation Bill passed by the Parliament, the Chief Election Commissioner will have full powers of re-appropriation.

06. Various economy instructions issued by the Finance Ministry from time to time will be communicated separately by the Finance Ministry to the Chief Election Commissioner, as is done in respect of the C&AG, Supreme Court etc.

07. The expenditure incurred by the Election Commission is subject to audit under the provisions of Article 149 of the Constitution read with the C&AG's Act, 1971.

The chief election commissioner was also empowered to create any post up to the rank of joint secretary. In short the Election Commission's financial powers were finally at par with those of the Supreme Court.

But the expenditure of the Election Commission even in 2002 was not—the position is the same today—charged upon the Consolidated Fund of India as was the expenditure of Parliament, or the Supreme Court, or the Comptroller and Auditor General, or the Union Public Service Commission. It was—and still is—voted expenditure and is subject to parliamentary debate. This was sought to be remedied in the Election Commission (Charging of Expenses on the Consolidated Fund of India) Bill, 1994, in the Lok Sabha but the bill eventually lapsed. And political parties have since not had the appetite to revive the matter.

7

Beginnings of Defiance

For the record, though, the first time the Election Commission had showed some spine was in the 1-Garhwal Parliamentary Constituency bye-election in 1981. Hemwati Nandan Bahuguna had been elected to the Lok Sabha from the same constituency in the General Elections of 1979. This was on an Indian National Congress (I) ticket. After the elections he had an ego problem with Indira Gandhi, then both prime minister and president of the INC (I). He resigned his seat after leaving the party, and was determined to contest the bye-election and win the seat again, but this time entirely on his own. This was really cocking a snook at Indira Gandhi while other Congressmen grovelled before her.

Enormous pressure was put on Sham Lal Shakdher, the chief election commissioner, not to hold the bye-election, and in any case, not to do so in a hurry. The bye-election was held up by natural causes, the constituency being snowbound in parts in winter. The weather having cleared, Shakdher shook the Congress off his back and decided to have the bye-election in May–June, 1981. The Congress pitted against Bahuguna the minister for hill development in

Uttar Pradesh and poured in all the state resources to somehow win this prestigious contest—de facto between Bahuguna and Indira Gandhi. Bahuguna was literally up against it. Police forces in considerable strength and secretly procured from Haryana had physically captured the constituency, much to the horror of the district magistrate and superintendent of police, Pauri. The deed was done so swiftly that even the Election Commission got to know about it only from a plethora of complaints of booth-capturing by the policemen from Haryana.

The commission's inquiry team visited the constituency and found the complaints largely substantiated. Having been discovered, the Indira Congress planned to cut its losses by urging repolls be confined to the polling stations about which specific complaints had been made. However the commission declared the poll in the entire constituency as void. In an historic order of 20 June 1981 the commission took the path-breaking stand that the electorate of the constituency was overawed by too much police—a lot of it from Haryana, with no local authority but with the sole purpose of electoral skulduggery—and this made a free and fair poll impossible. But the Congress continued to obstruct and flung a lot of chaff: the onslaught of the monsoon, school and university examinations, wintry conditions . . . A year after, the repoll in the bye-election was duly completed. This was just one month before Shakdher retired.

Having thrown the gauntlet at Indira Gandhi over the Garhwal bye-election, the commission under Shakdher was determined to press further its new-found independence in the use of the electronic voting machine. The First and Second General Elections in 1951-52 and 1957 respectively were held under the balloting system of voting. Under this system each candidate was allotted a separate ballot box bearing his symbol, and every voter was given a standard ballot paper which he dropped into the ballot box of the candidate of his choice. With the Third General Election in 1962 the voting system adopted was the marking system of voting, still in vogue. Under this arrangement a ballot paper containing the names of all the contesting candidates was given to the voter and he was required to put a mark on or near the symbol of the candidate he chose to vote for.

In a country with hundreds of millions of voters it seemed churlish to persist with ballot paper and ballot box—a primitive, and labour and paper-intensive system which, incidentally, carried with it a not insignificant percentage of invalid votes, the result of indeterminate marking. Electronic voting would not only be brisker but more efficient. And there would be no invalid votes. But the idea had to be converted, and Electronics Corporation of India Ltd. (ECIL), Hyderabad, was given the task in 1977. Within a couple of years they had a prototype of an electronic voting machine which the Election Commission demonstrated to the political parties on 6 August 1980. The reaction was generally favourable, and even Indira Gandhi seemed satisfied. In the meanwhile Bharat Electronics Ltd. (BEL), Bangalore, also developed a voting machine prototype. The two organizations then met frequently and evolved a common design. The commission took the Government of India's permission to buy a few machines to experiment with. Relevant departments were roped in and the price of each machine was fixed at Rs. 7,500. The government's sanction was for 350 machines, orders for 250 of which were placed on ECIL, the remaining orders being given to BEL. Supplies were to be completed by April 1982.

The commission notified in June 1981 its intention to the government to use the machines on a trial basis in some of the approaching bye-elections to the state legislative assemblies as well as in the General Elections to the Metropolitan Council of Delhi. Parri passu, it also requested the government to initiate amendments to the Representation of the People Act, 1951 to provide for the use of electronic voting machines instead of ballot boxes and ballot papers. The government, in an about-face, maintained a studied silence. This gave rise to speculation that some of Indira Gandhi's busy advisers had counselled her that the machines were an insidious attempt at eliminating the then profitable practice of stuffing ballot boxes. A reminder in April 1982 enclosing draft amendments to the RPA, 1951 got no response. Later in April 1982 the commission wrote again stressing the urgency of the proposed amendments in the context of its decision to use the fifty EVMs then available with it in the Parur bye-election in Kerala scheduled for 19 May 1982. While the commission queried the government on the progress, if any, on the required legislation, there was also a veiled warning that in the event of the amendment not being accomplished before 8 May, the commission might examine an alternative course of action to use the fifty EVMs. From its behaviour, the government had neither received nor noticed anything.

Shakdher, having inspired the invention of the voting machine and due to retire in June 1982, was going to use the machine in the Parur bye-election, come what may. The commission drew upon its plenary powers under Article 324 of the Constitution and brought out a notification detailing directions and procedures on the use of the machine. (The infallible draftsman then was Surinder Kumar Mendiratta—now legal counsel and author of *How India Votes: Election Law, Practice and Procedure*—and he remains so.) The experiment succeeded, parties, candidates and voters hailing the neatness and brevity of the exercise. But there was one exception—candidate A.C. Jose, one of the losers, who challenged the result of the election in the Kerala High Court.

In June 1982 Ram Kishen Trivedi took over as chief election commissioner and decided to use electronic voting machines more extensively. A request to the government for 400 additional machines and a reminder on the required amendment to the law followed. Trivedi also got impatient and repeated the reminder in September. He expressed his intention to use the machine in the ensuing elections in Nagaland and Delhi. Another reminder and then a meaningless reply from the Ministry of Law to the effect that the commission's proposal was under consideration and that the decision taken would be communicated in due course—the typical waffle that normally went to an individual petitioner who was too insistent about a reply. But this was not the sort of response that ought to have gone to a constitutional body charged with conducting elections on a crucial proposal aimed at improving the electoral process.

With the government clearly temporizing the commission went ahead with the use of EVMs—in ten more assembly constituencies. These were Northern Angami I (Nagaland), Shadnagar (Andhra Pradesh), Shanthinagar (Karnataka), Banmalipur and Charilam (Tripura), Sarojini Nagar, Gole Market and Delhi Cantt. (Delhi), Roing (Arunachal Pradesh) and Chandi (Bihar).

The machines suffered a setback in March 1984, the Supreme Court having struck down their use in the Parur assembly constituency in Kerala on the appeal filed against the order of the Kerala High Court (*A.C. Jose Vs. Sivan Pillai and Others* 71 ELR 23) which had upheld the use of the machines by the commission in exercise of its powers under Article 324. The Supreme Court in *A.C. Jose Vs. Sivan Pillai and Others* AIR 1984 8C 921 took the view that the law provided for conducting elections with ballot papers and ballot boxes and the commission could not use EVMs in the absence of enabling statutory provisions.

Thus the Election Commission had effectively circumvented a prevaricating government to implement a crucial piece of electoral reform but was stopped short by the Court which went strictly by the law. The necessary amendment in the Representation of the People Act 1951 was passed only in December 1988, Indira Gandhi having had nothing to do with it in her lifetime but Rajiv Gandhi, prime minister then, seeming to be more receptive.

*

The defiance continued. Chief election commissioners, retired bureaucrats purring with the pleasure of re-employment, were supposed to be convenient. Came elections and the government told them when to fix the dates. This comfortable domestic arrangement suddenly so fell apart in the presidential election of 1987 that the Election Commission of India is now perhaps the only one in the world which does not consult the government about election schedules. Rajiv Gandhi as prime minister and Giani Zail Singh as President were anathema to each other, and Zail Singh had to be prevented from winning a second term as an opposition-sponsored candidate. Every vote counted as the President is elected by an electoral college of members of Parliament and of the legislative assemblies of the states. Zail Singh's term came to an end on 24 July and the elections to the Haryana legislative assembly, which was to complete its five-year term on 24 June, were due in May–June 1987. But it was expected that the Congress, then ruling Haryana, would get a drubbing. So Rajiv Gandhi wanted the chief election commissioner (the late Rudrabhatla Venkata Surya Peri-Sastri) to hold the presidential elections before the Haryana assembly elections. If this was not possible, the schedule, at least for the presidential election, should be so fixed that the first stage in the electoral process—the nomination of candidates—was over before the Haryana results were declared so as to deprive Zail Singh of any encouragement from their outcome. Peri-Sastri was pressured in a variety of ways, friends, acquaintances and others holding him in high esteem being made to persuade him to the government's objective. His personal records in the Ministry of Law, where he had been secretary of the Legislative Department, and his income and property returns were trawled for possible irregularities and deficiencies. Sastri withstood the tide, though not entirely on his own. He took his troubles to a temple and came out unburdened and strengthened in his resolve to resist. The presidential election was notified on 10 June 1987, the last date for filing nominations being 24 June. By then the Haryana elections were already over and the Congress had lost, the opposition having taken over the state on 20 June 1987.

8

EC Survives First Packing

Whatever the Election Commission had grown up to as an institution stood perilously in danger with its sudden conversion into a multi-member commission in October 1989. Not a multi-member commission per se, which was provided for by Article 324 of the Constitution, but one appointed just before the Lok Sabha elections of December 1989 to dilute Peri-Sastri's independence. It was clearly meant to help the Congress party to retain power. The Constituent Assembly had dreaded the political Executive's control of the Election Commission (Indira Gandhi had earlier temporarily disabled the Supreme Court by having her nominees supersede their superior colleagues) and this had at last come to pass.

In his order of 7 October 1989, the President, under Article 324(2), decided to have two election commissioners in addition to the chief election commissioner. This was followed by a notification of 16 October appointing S.S. Dhanoa and V.S. Seigell as the two election commissioners with immediate effect. The same day, rules under Article 324(5) regulated their conditions of service and tenure of office—the tenure would be five years or until the age of sixty-five, whichever was earlier.

The officers of the Election Commission recall the events of 1989 very vividly. When the Janata Dal wanted the wheel as their symbol they had to cite many precedents to get it. They had brought a whole battery of artists and the first sketch was of a wheel with twenty-four spokes. This was promptly rejected as something too close to the Ashok Chakra. Dhanoa supported by Seigell gave them only three spokes, but somebody objected saying it looked like the sign of the Youth Congress. Thereafter Dhanoa just doubled the number to six. After which, while he and the Janata leaders were trooping out of the room, the late Devi Lal said, 'We know what you have been up to, we shall be back in a couple of months and you will be the first to be thrown out.'

The results of the Lok Sabha elections confirmed Devi Lal's prognostication. With V.P. Singh as prime minister, the President on 1 January 1990 was equally pleased to revert the Election Commission to a single-member institution and rescinded the notifications of 7 and 16 October. Dhanoa approached the Supreme Court against the President's decision asserting that an election commissioner once appointed continued for his full term of five years, and that the President had no power to abbreviate it. It was also contended that by removing the two election commissioners the President had eroded the independence of the Election Commission.

A division bench of the Supreme Court (M.H. Kania and P.B. Sawant, JJ) saw no merit in Dhanoa's case and dismissed the petition. The court said there was no need for the posts of election commissioners when Dhanoa and Seigell were appointed. Besides, since the role of the election commissioner was not defined, abolishing the posts not only did not compromise the independence of the Election

Commission but contributed to its smooth and effective functioning. An observation was also made that the creation and abolition of posts was the prerogative of the Executive, Article 324(2) leaving it to the President to fix and appoint as many election commissioners as he might from time to time determine. Since the posts had been abolished the associated service rules had gone defunct.

The Supreme Court had fortunately put paid to the attempt to pack the commission. But it also drove a nail in the coffin to deter any potential future attempt—the intention of the framers of the Constitution was to have the chief election commissioner not as *primus interpares* but in a distinctly higher position. The distinction between the chief election commissioner and election commissioners was then written into law—the Chief Election Commissioner and other Election Commissioners (Conditions of Service) Act, 1991. The chief election commissioner was to retire at sixty-five and enjoy the salary and perks of a judge of the Supreme Court while the election commissioners were to retire at sixty-two and to be given the salary and perks of a high court judge.

9

Model Code of Conduct

The most enduring impact on Indian elections and the political Executive had been made by the Model Code of Conduct—usually called just the Model Code—for the guidance of political parties and candidates. It was begotten in the 1960s but it became effective only in the early '90s. In between it underwent fundamental changes.

The election law—in the Representation of the People Acts, 1950 and 1951 and the Indian Penal Code—is about corrupt practices and other electoral offences and like every other law it addresses itself to individual offenders. But at election time the main offenders are the political parties. So the Model Code of Conduct was required to fill the vacuum. Initially it was an agreed set of dos and don'ts for the February 1960 legislative assembly elections and it was hammered out by the Kerala state administration together with the political parties. It also included a lot of guidelines on meetings and processions, speeches and slogans, posters and placards. There was little change in the content till 1979, but quite clearly there were increasing difficulties about its observance. In 1967, when there were the first signs of the breaking up of the one-party Congress monolith, parties had to be appealed to to follow the Code of

Conduct. By 1974 the Election Commission had sought to get the code implemented through a committee under the district magistrate. Soon after there was an end to the paternalistic system which everybody had hitherto admired. People had seen how State institutions had been abused during the Emergency and no longer trusted the government of the day either in Delhi or in the states. After hearing complaints from the political parties the Election Commission in 1979 included a whole section on the party in power—basically interdictions. By the early 1990s the further disintegration of the Congress, the equalization of the parties, the increased competition, the need for coalitions, the importance of small parties in the coalitions, manipulations to secure a majority through bribery or defection, the perception of politics as the most productive source of wealth for anyone criminally inclined and the pandering to vote banks had made Indian elections the most violent and noxious events possible. That is when the Election Commission was forced to pitch into the ruling party—in other words the government of the day—to try and reduce it to the level of its competitors. With some additions the negatives for the party in power had assumed formidable proportions:

> The party in power whether at the Centre or in the State or States concerned, shall ensure that no cause is given for any complaint that it has used its official position for the purposes of its election campaign and in particular —
>
> (i) (a) The Ministers shall not combine their official visit with electioneering work and shall also not make use of official machinery or personnel during the electioneering work;

(b) Government transport including official aircraft, vehicles, machinery and personnel shall not be used for furtherance of the interest of the party in power;

(ii) Public places such as maidans etc., for holding election meetings, and use of helipads for air-flights in connection with elections shall not be monopolised by itself. Other parties and candidates shall be allowed the use of such places and facilities on the same terms and conditions on which they are used by the party in power;

(iii) Rest houses, dak-bungalows or other Government accommodation shall not be monopolised by the party in power or its candidates and such accommodation shall be allowed to be used by other parties and candidates in a fair manner but no party or candidate shall use or be allowed to use such accommodation (including premises appertaining thereto) as a campaign office or for holding any public meeting for the purposes of election propaganda;

(iv) No issue of advertisement at the cost of public exchequer in the newspapers and other media and the misuse of official mass media during the election period for partisan coverage of political news, and publicity regarding achievements with a view to furthering the prospects of the party in power shall be scrupulously avoided.

(v) Ministers and other authorities shall not sanction grants/payments out of discretionary funds from the time elections are announced by the Commission; and

(vi) From the time elections are announced by the

Commission, Ministers and other authorities shall not—

(a) announce any financial grants in any form or promises thereof; or

(b) (except civil servants) lay foundation stones etc. of projects or schemes of any kind; or

(c) make any promise of construction of roads, provision of drinking water facilities etc.; or

(d) make any ad-hoc appointments in Government, Public Undertakings etc.

which may have the effect of influencing the voters in favour of the party in power.

Note: The Commission shall announce the date of any election which shall be a date ordinarily not more than three weeks prior to the date on which the notification is likely to be issued in respect of such elections.

(vii) Ministers of Central or State Government shall not enter any polling station or place of counting except in their capacity as a candidate or voter or authorised agent.

Tours of Ministers

From the date of announcement and till the completion of elections, Ministers (of Central or State Government) are not to undertake official tours to any constituency from where election has been announced by the Commission, except in situations of failure of law and order, natural calamity, or any other emergency requiring the personal presence of Ministers.

Ministers are also not to lay foundation stones, etc. of projects of any kind. This may be done by civil servants. New schemes/projects are not to be launched. However, ongoing projects may continue.

Misuse of official aircraft and vehicles

Official vehicles are not to be used for election related travel during elections. There is an exception in the case of Prime Minister and other personalities, whose security requirements are governed by any statutory provisions. In the case of government aircraft, only the Prime Minister in office is permitted to use the same.

MPs Local Area Development Scheme (MPLAD)

After announcement of elections, fresh funds under the MPLAD Scheme cannot be released. Work for any MPLAD Scheme cannot be started during election period.

In September 2002—when the Kashmir Assembly elections took place—was the Model Code of Conduct, which had no statutory backing, recognized by the Court? The code had been to several high courts and the Supreme Court on issues like when it should apply and which items were justifiable and which were not. But no one had questioned the need for such a code. So by implication it had received the recognition of the courts.

After all the litigation how much of it remained? The strongest reaction had been against the directions putting curbs on the official tours of ministers during election time. By the directives of 31 December 1993, ministers, non-official chairmen and directors of government bodies visiting a district or constituency going into elections, after elections had been announced, were not to be provided official transport or declared as state guests. They were also not to convene any official meetings or use government vehicles or take their personal staff with them. They could go there only as ordinary citizens, not to be taken cognisance of by local officialdom. The sole exception was the prime minister whose security requirements allowed him to use all state facilities from accommodation to motor vehicles to aircraft.

Tamil Nadu was the first to take offence requesting the commission to exempt the chief minister from the directives. Having got a negative the state government put in a writ petition before the Supreme Court saying the impugned directives would seriously jeopardize the security of the chief minister in election campaigning since there were serious threats to her life from extremist and terrorist groups. Besides, the chief minister was entitled to security arrangements under the Tamil Nadu Special Security Group Act 1993, and the state government was obliged to provide them. The Court ruled that it was not quite right to confine security to the prime minister. Besides, the Election Commission would have to take note of statutory provisions. However, the security requirements were not to be 'so manifestly and unduly excessive as to amount to promotion, indirectly, of partisan electoral interests'.

Andhra Pradesh followed and the subject of the exemption prayed for was again the chief minister. But the writ petition was withdrawn after the Election Commission had revised its directives in the light of the Supreme Court's order on the Tamil Nadu case.

Two years later the Election Commission directives got even more stringent to meet a situation where ministers were touring the constituencies and electioneering under the garb of some other official work. The new directives said all tours of Union and state ministers were banned from the date of announcing the Lok Sabha elections till these had ended.

The directives were quietly imbibed in the parliamentary elections of 1996 and 1998. But in the same elections in 1999 the Union government wanted a relaxation on the tours of Central ministers citing important meetings, at times with foreign delegations, outside Delhi. Also the Kargil conflict in Jammu and Kashmir required touring outside Delhi. The Election Commission allowed the tours subject to the secretaries of the concerned ministries certifying to the chief secretaries of the states to be visited that the visits were purely official and unavoidable in the public interest. The Union ministers were specifically discouraged from official visits to their home states and particularly their constituencies.

Since ministers of the states were not exempt one of the Uttar Pradesh ministers filed a discrimination writ petition before the Supreme Court. Another writ petition was by one of the members of the state legislative council. The Supreme Court noted that the directives had provided for tours by ministers in charge of concerned departments/state chief ministers in exceptional circumstances like failure of law and order or natural calamity 'or such emergency requiring personal presence of such ministers/Chief Ministers for the purpose of supervising operations'. Since for such official visits the ministers/chief ministers would be allowed to use government vehicles the court chose not to interfere. Ad hoc appointments by government had also been the subject of litigation. In the run up to the Delhi assembly elections in 1993 the Delhi Administration, after the announcement of the elections, appointed some non-official members to the Delhi Agricultural Marketing Board under the Delhi Agricultural Produce Marketing (Regulation) Act, 1976. On complaint the Election Commission asked the administration to cancel the appointments and this was complied with. However, the aggrieved parties approached the Delhi High Court. The court upheld the action by the commission. It observed* that 'the Election Commission is fully competent to lay down any guidelines or issue appropriate directions for the purpose of accomplishing the paramount object of free and fair election as contemplated in the Constitution of India, and all concerned are bound to follow them in letter and spirit. This is the pith and substance of Article 324. We are, therefore, of the view that the Election Commission was within its jurisdiction to take cognisance of the complaint made against the nominations.'

Nevertheless the court orders did not disturb the status quo holding† 'that the direction on behalf of the Election Commission was issued without application of mind of the Commission and that the decision was taken by the Secretary to the Commission at his own level in excess of his jurisdiction'.

In another case, in Uttar Pradesh, where the director general of police's service had been extended beyond retirement during the operation of the Code of Conduct, the Central Administrative Tribunal held that the code did not cover 'extension in service'.

The courts have therefore at times questioned the application and manner of application of the code but have not whittled it down in any way. When did the code begin

---

*Judgement dated 5 April 1996 in CWP 593 and 1633 of 1994
†*Supra*

to operate and end? This aspect has generated more heated debate than any other, the reason being that—especially in assembly elections—prohibitory directions from the Election Commission reduce the political Executive to a nullity. In the constitutional scheme of things the power of the state was to be distributed only amongst the political Executive, Legislature and Judiciary. So where did this upstart of an Election Commission or controller of governments during elections come from? Formally, it was debatable whether the Model Code ought to have been recognized, but since it had, could its duration be reduced to the minimum?

While the Election Commission maintained that the Model Code applied from the date of announcement of elections and ended after counting was over, the Union government and some state governments considered that the application should be from the date of notification of the elections. In 1994 the Andhra Pradesh government approached the Supreme Court, but since the bye-election in Kurnool was over and done with in the meantime, the petitioners withdrew the petition and the Court disposed of the matter without any ruling on the question raised in the petition.

In another writ petition by the Telugu Desam party before the Andhra Pradesh High Court, a single judge made an interim observation that the code would be from the date of notification. The Election Commission contested this observation before a division bench of the same high court. In this case also the election had gone by and the writ petition had been withdrawn and the case disposed of without any decision on the vital question.

On the other hand the Punjab and Haryana High Court in *Harbans Singh Jalal Vs. Union of India and Others* in relation to the state assembly elections of 1996 concluded that the Model Code operated from the date of announcement of the elections. The Union government was unhappy with the decision and appealed to the Supreme Court. The matter ended with a compromise between the Union of India and the Election Commission to the effect that the code would operate from the date of announcement but that the duration of the interval between the announcement and the notification would not normally exceed three weeks.

Union and state governments as well as the media—given the dates by which the reconstituted Parliament/state legislatures had to be convened, the impossibility of elections during the monsoon and in certain mountainous areas during winter—had learnt to gauge fairly accurately when the dates of the elections were likely to be. With a period of just twenty-one days between the announcement of elections and the notification, governments had also learnt how to put into effect their election-influencing appointments and sanctions just before the Election Commission announced the elections. To that extent, therefore, the abbreviated announcement–notification interval had allowed governments to partially circumvent the Code of Conduct. But if the code had operated only from the date of notification, the other portion of it—by virtue of the brevity of its period of operation—would also have been rendered less effective.

Without statutory backing, how had the observance of the code been ensured? Till the Tenth General Elections to the Lok Sabha in 1991 the Election Commission had left the code to voluntary observance. From then onwards it started showing displeasure over the conduct of dignitaries and even censuring them in public. One of the conspicuous examples was of a governor who went back to his hometown in Madhya Pradesh—where one of his sons was a candidate—

and who was not only in the thick of the election campaign but was also alleged to have misused the Madhya Pradesh government machinery. The impact of the censure was such that he had to resign.

What served much better was the cancellation of elections on serious breaches of the code. The Kalka assembly bye-lection in Haryana in 1993 was cancelled when the chief minister announced new development schemes for the area after the election had been announced. The chief minister's son was one of the contestants. There was a similar cancellation of the Ranipet assembly bye-election in Tamil Nadu when the chief minister announced new schemes. No government thereafter was so obtuse as to commit the same kind of error. Since the Election Commission had stopped consulting the government on the dates for the elections in protection of the Model Code, there had been a prolonged battle of wits between the Election Commission on one side and governments on the other. The object of the Election Commission was to expand the interval between the announcement and the notification so that there would be no new schemes and appointments within any proximity of the elections. The governments had tried to minimize the interval and bring the appointments and sanctions as near to the elections as possible. But until the interval was fixed at twenty-one days it was a question of whether the Election Commission could get in an announcement of the elections earlier, or the governments their sanctions and appointments.

Would it have helped the commission if the Code of Conduct had been made into law? The initial response was yes. But it was soon realized that conducting elections, though occasionally involving quasi-legislative functions and more often quasi-judicial functions, was intrinsically an Executive task. Mention has been made about the penal provisions of the Representation of the People Act and Indian Penal Code. But looking at it from the perspective of the Election Commission, there was no point in prosecuting a person after he had committed the offence. What was required was a mechanism to take preventive action or to correct the course of events, insulating it from aberrating factors. And the code as it was, was reasonably effective for this purpose. Of course, if the Representation of the People Act could have been so restructured as to include the anticipatory and corrective aspects—roughly on the lines of the Code of Criminal Procedure—it might have been useful writing the Code of Conduct into the law.

But the law in India had been remarkably negligent of political parties and their doings. The Constitution took thirty-five years to take cognisance of political parties—not a word about political parties till it had to ban defections in 1985 and wrote this up in the Tenth Schedule. The Representation of the People Act, 1951 was under great compulsion to be slightly less remiss. After Indira Gandhi had been convicted of electoral corruption the Representation of the People Act was amended to exclude the expenditure of political parties from the expenditure limits of the individual candidates. But these were all oblique references to political parties as though they were abstract entities. With all the rhetoric on the 'criminalization of politics' Indian electoral legislation had taken no cognisance of the primacy of political parties in the election process, much less their increasingly abominable conduct. That they were live, and in fact rather robust players in the democratic process that had to be grappled with every day in the year was in a way recognized only in the 15 June 1989 amendment of the Representation of the People Act which in Section 29A dealt with the Election Commission's registration of political parties.

10

The Commission Asserts Itself

B ut the most audacious decision of the commission—of
2 August 1993—was to shut down the electoral section
of the constitutional machinery until its impasse with the
Union government had been resolved. The issues were
disciplining officers 'deemed to be on deputation' with the
Election Commission, the commission's requirement of
officers for election duty and its power to direct state and
Central governments to deploy such Central and state police
forces as were considered necessary to achieve free and fair
elections.

The August 1993 order, dictated by Secretary Surinder
Kumar Mendiratta, typed on the computer by Deputy
Election Commissioner D.S. Bagga and touched up by
Deputy Election Commissioner Viswanathan was a tour de
force in logic and assumed reasonableness. And it was in
just the right injured and sanctimonious tone required for
litigation at the time (not that it has changed much since).
On the first issue the Constituent Assembly was
uncompromising about free and fair elections and an
independent Election Commission. At the same time, to
save on costs and duplication, it did not allow separate field
staff for the commission. Which inevitably led to the

commission's dependence for conducting elections on the political Executive and the government servants at its command, many of whom had become partisan. To deal with them and those charged with dereliction of duty, Section 13CC of the Representation of the People Act, 1950 and Section 28A of the same Act, 1951 had given ample disciplinary authority to the Election Commission.

Unfortunately the Cabinet secretary had put a roadblock in the case of some defaulting officers deputed for observers' duty in 1992. On their explanations he declined to take action but carefully mystified the issue, thus: 'Due priority will always be given by the Government to sparing officers for election work. However, circumstances may arise occasionally, when Government is unable to spare particular officers of the Departments. Government are being informed that whenever such eventualities arise the Election Commission should be informed and alternative arrangements suggested in advance.' The commission countered to the effect that if any officer was unable to perform his electoral duties he or the government should seek exemption from the commission and offer a replacement. If this position was accepted by the government the matter would be treated as closed; with no reply from the government the commission took disciplinary action against the defaulting officers and passed necessary orders asking the Department of Personnel to put the orders in their annual confidential report dossiers. The response was that only the Union government or state governments as disciplinary authorities were competent to take action against the officers concerned. The findings of the chief election commissioner could only be regarded as preliminary inquiries on the basis of which the officers could comment and enable the Department of Personnel to take a final view of the matter.

On the second issue, while the commission asserted that under Article 324 (6) it was to assess staff requirements for its constitutional obligations, the government was equally clear that it was up to it to determine 'the quantum of staff necessary'.

The related issue arose out of anticipated law and order problems of a serious nature in the 22-Palani Parliamentary constituency and 34-Ranipet assembly constituency bye-elections in Tamil Nadu. The commission had directed the Government of India to deploy adequate Central police forces in the two constituencies without waiting for a request from the state government, since the state government was playing down the situation and was not likely to make the request. The two governments were also to report compliance by a certain date. In the event the Government of India provided some Central police forces in response to a state government message but kept the Election Commission out of the picture. The government's view was that law and order was a state subject and it was up to the state government to make a demand for paramilitary or other forces. This was not the jurisdiction of the Election Commission. On the other hand the commission considered that as part of its responsibility for free and fair elections it was obliged to give directions on the deployment of additional police forces where the situation demanded.

Since there was a deadlock on all issues and the chief election commissioner's meeting the prime minister had not borne fruit 'the Commission does not find itself in a position to carry out its constitutional obligations in the manner envisaged by the makers of the Constitution, and has accordingly decided that all and every election under its control, including biennial and bye-elections to the Council of States, bye-elections to the State Legislative Councils, bye-elections to the House of the People and bye-elections to the State Legislative Assemblies, as have been announced or notified or are in progress, shall remain postponed until further orders'. The commission would not 'take any action to hold any elections for which it has authority and responsibility until the Government of India accepts and announces its willingness in unequivocal language to abide by the provisions of the Constitution and the law relating to Elections, and the entire work will be resumed as soon as the Government of India communicates the same'.

Since the Government of India refused to stir the Election Commission filed a writ petition in the Supreme Court primarily on the point of who could take disciplinary action on officers and staff doing elections and election-related duty. But relief was sought on the other issues as well. The urgency of the matter was such that there was a hearing on 10 August 1993, and by 14 October the Court had already directed that the representatives of the Ministry of Home Affairs and state governments and the directors general of the Central paramilitary forces should sit with the commission and take a collective decision on the requirement of observers and the deployment of Central police forces in states going to the polls.

Since then the Election Commission's demands for Central paramilitary forces—after discussions with the Union home secretary—and for observers to the Department of Personnel—not merely in terms of number but also of particular officers specially selected for the purpose—have been met. Contrary to resisting the deployment of Central paramilitary forces, the states have gone to the opposite extreme and demanded much more police force from outside than could possibly be provided any time an election was in sight. There were at least two reasons for this development.

Opposition parties had lost confidence in the neutrality of the state police, and over the years financial constraints had prevented the augmentation of the state forces to the level of their requirements. In the event the commission had become the dominant partner in the conduct of elections in the states.

The hard residue of disciplining officers deemed on deputation with the Election Commission remained with the Supreme Court. What the acid correspondence between Chief Election Commissioner Seshan and Cabinet Secretary Rajgopal couldn't dissolve, a peg or two of whisky and an evening's conviviality between Ram Jethmalani, Union law minister, and Manohar Gill did, or at least partly. The compromise was in the following terms*:

That the disciplinary functions of the Election Commission of India over officers, staff and police deputed to perform election duty during election period shall extend to:

(a) suspending any officer/official/police personnel for insubordination or dereliction of duty;

(b) substituting any officer/official/police personnel by another such person, and returning the substituted individual to the cadre to which he belongs, with appropriate report on his conduct;

(c) making recommendation to the competent authority, for taking disciplinary action, for any act of insubordination or dereliction of duty, while on election duty. Such recommendation shall be promptly acted upon by the disciplinary authority,

---

Landmark Judgements on Election Law, Vol.III, published by ECI, pp.54-58

and action taken will be communicated to the Election Commission, within a period of six months from the date of Election Commission's recommendations.

The statement also mentioned, 'The Government of India will advise the State Governments that they too should follow the above principles and decisions, since a large number of election officials are under their administrative control.'

The attorney general met the standing counsels for the state governments and the governments of Andhra Pradesh, Maharashtra, Mizoram, Tamil Nadu and Tripura accepted the terms in toto. The Supreme Court, after a joint application by the Election Commission and Union of India enclosing the terms of settlement, accordingly disposed of the case.* But the settlement itself was leaky. Most of the states had not accepted it, leaving scope for future litigation.

The Election Commission asserted itself elsewhere. The Constituent Assembly very wisely had decided on a permanent Election Commission working through the given field machinery. But it had not thought of a permanent electoral establishment at each state headquarters. The Representation of the People Acts 1950 and 1951 did— under a chief electoral officer. The preparation and revision of electoral rolls and conduct of elections were to be under the supervision, direction and control of the chief electoral officer as representative of the Election Commission.

The chief electoral officer was initially routinely appointed by the state governments under the provisions of the Representation of the People (Preparation of Electoral Rolls)

Landmark Judgements on Election Law, Vol.III, published by ECI, pp.54–58

Rules, 1950. Since he was to function under the Election Commission his appointment was expected to be made with its concurrence. The Representation of the People Acts 1950 and '51 were amended in 1956 to that effect.

Theoretically the chief electoral officer could be from another cadre but in practice he has always been from the cadre of the state in which he held that position. At one time chief electoral officers were part-time senior civil servants or judicial officers and transfers were made without consulting the commission. From the 1980s most governments had been made to agree to sending a panel of three or four names of officers of the rank of secretary to the state government for the commission to make a selection. But as late as 1993 there was a serious stand-off between the Election Commission and the government of West Bengal in the implementation of this scheme. The state government reneged on sparing the services of the officer selected, making the commission select a substitute from a fresh panel. But the officer so selected was reluctant to join, citing health reasons. The Election Commission, Seshan, that is, not only refused to make another selection but suspended correspondence with the state for a couple of years. The state government was compelled to approach the Calcutta High Court, but in the process had to assure the court that it would spare the full-time services of the officer selected from a panel of names submitted by the state. Since then, in many cases, the commission had not considered names submitted by the state governments acceptable and had proposed its own names and secured the state government's consent. Also, the disintegration of state administrations, the risks of working under devious ministers as well as of vindictiveness with change of governments had, by comparison with normal state postings, made the chief electoral officer's post quite desirable.

Much conflict with the political Executive was also generated by the issue of identity cards. Though the voting right is derived from the electoral roll, the voter is required to be identified. And so the need for the identity card in a context where impersonation had characterized Indian elections since independence and was visibly on the increase. Till the identity card there was no document to check the voter's identity beyond the slip given to him by one of the political parties to show that he was so and so in the electoral roll and had to vote in such and such polling station. To prevent multiple voting, indelible ink was applied to a voter's finger nail but if he had voted before the ink was dry he could rub off the ink and vote again with the connivance of the polling staff.

Understandably all political parties in power were against the use of the identity card and took no interest in getting it made. Against this background the Election Commission's order announced on 28 August 1993, that voters all over India barring Jammu and Kashmir would be supplied identity cards with photographs and that no polling for elections to Parliament or the state assemblies would take place after 1 January 1995 unless all eligible voters had been given identity cards, was patently rash. Though the order did not hold when challenged in court, it terrified the states into activity and legitimized the currency of the identity card in most parts of the country.

At the Second General Elections in 1957 impersonation had already been recognized as a widespread menace. In response to the demand for identity cards the commission experimented with identity cards in the Calcutta South-West Parliamentary constituency bye-election. For this an amendment had to be made in Section 61 of the Representation of the People Act, 1951 and in the 1960 Rules and 1961 Rules.

Whereas Rule 28 of the 1960 Rules allowed the Election Commission to issue identity cards only in a constituency within a municipal area, the Registration of Electors (Amendment) Rules, 1969, allowed the commission to do so in any constituency or part thereof.

Against an electorate of 3,42,000 in the Calcutta constituency, 2,13,600 voters were photographed and 2,10,000 voters got their identity cards. Women still resisted being photographed and many voters were too busy to be found at home. The experiment was not encouraging.

Sikkim, which became a state within the Indian Union in 1975, seemed to be a tempting target—with an electorate of just 125,000. The Sikkim assembly elections were in 1979, and once again with every back bent for the programme many electors had not got their cards. It was also tried in Meghalaya and Nagaland with similar results. The identity card programme was therefore shelved in 1983-84.

The commission tried a different tack in 1986, persuading state governments to use electoral identity cards as multi-purpose cards for bank and post office accounts, essential commodities distribution, public health schemes and other purposes. The state governments were requested to consider this again in 1992. Cards were required to be distributed free, but they didn't come free to the state government, and while they were toting up the costs and wondering where the money would come from, Seshan sprung the August 1993 order on them.

The states tried to push the entire cost to the Centre while the government was only prepared for a pilot project of two or three constituencies per state. The confusion was resolved in a meeting taken by the prime minister in September 1994. The decision was the costs would be equally shared by the Centre and the states and the badly off states would be given advances to begin the work.

But the West Bengal government had already filed a writ petition in the Calcutta High Court against the commission's notification of August 1993. The petition was admitted and a single judge stayed the impugned order, whereas a similar petition filed before another single judge in the Kerala High Court was dismissed. The petitioner in Kerala filed a writ appeal before a division bench. The Election Commission then approached the Supreme Court for a transfer of the two cases to itself and for vacating the stay order of the Calcutta High Court. The stay order was vacated with the direction that the writ petition be disposed of by a division bench of the Calcutta High Court. At the same time the single judge of the Calcutta High Court sent a contempt notice to Seshan, the then chief election commissioner, for having violated the stay order and written to other state governments like Andhra Pradesh and Karnataka to adhere to the commission's deadline in issuing the identity cards. This time the commission petitioned the Supreme Court for a stay of the contempt notice. The court allowed the case in Calcutta to be transferred to itself and directed that if there were any other similar writ petitions with other high courts these would automatically stand transferred as well.

The identity cards were all required to be issued by 31 December 1994. Since assembly elections were to be held in the first quarter of the calendar year 1995 in Bihar and Orissa, the Election Commission announced the elections on 8 December 1994. In para 6 of the press note it was stipulated, 'A poll in any of these States will not be taken without the supply of electoral ID cards to all eligible electors. The State Government will be called upon to furnish the certificate the photo ID cards have been supplied to all eligible electors.'

Since neither state could furnish a certificate of that kind it was believed that the proposed elections would not happen. Orissa was the first to panic and petitioned the Supreme Court to direct the commission not to hold back the election because cards had not been issued to every elector. Bihar followed. In the preliminary hearing on 17 January 1995 the Election Commission told the court that para 6 of the press note of 8 December 1994 would not operate against Orissa where 86 per cent of the voters had been covered by identity cards. Bihar, however, was a wilful defaulter. Bihar's reply was the commission had not taken into account that state's economic and social conditions in ramming the programme through. Besides, the Election Commission could not hold up elections or even threaten to do so just because identity cards had not been issued. The court took an undertaking from the commission that it would not hold up elections in Bihar. For its part, the commission requested that the court demand an undertaking from Bihar that it would issue the cards by September 1995. The state's counsel was instead allowed four weeks to seek instructions from the government about such an undertaking. Strangely the Election Commission went to the opposite extreme and did the elections on schedule without using identity cards at all.

In the years to follow, significant progress in identity card distribution had been registered in states like Gujarat, Haryana, Karnataka, Orissa and West Bengal. The commission took the next decisive step in the implementation of the identity card programme when it conducted the Haryana assembly elections in January–February 2000. Since 88 per cent of the electors had got identity cards—and some of the leeway could be accounted for by dead or shifted voters—it was safe to assume that in reality nearly all the electors had been given cards. Therefore, the commission insisted on identity cards for identification. However, since this was the first time that identity cards were being demanded from the voters and a few of them might not be having cards, other documents were also allowed, such as passports, driving licences, ration cards, Central and state government identity cards, similar cards from public sector undertakings, local bodies, industrial houses . . . (The same procedure was adopted in the bye-elections of May 2000).

In the Haryana elections nearly 80 per cent of the voters produced their identity cards. The commission placed the facts before the Supreme Court and also showed that there was progress in nearly all the states. The court took note of this and having considered that the petitions had become infructuous in the changed circumstances, closed the matter.

11

EC's Second Packing
Survives Litigation

Nothing, however, could deter the Executive from a second attempt at undermining an Election Commission which from the Government of India's point of view had grown too big for its shoes. In *T.N. Seshan Vs. Union of India and Others* [Writ Petition (Civil) No.805 of 1993 decided on 14 July 1995]* in the Supreme Court, Seshan attributed a series of decisions and actions taken by him as the cause for the Union government's second packing of the commission (he, of course, did not know it was coming, just as he supposedly knew nothing about Dhanoa's and Seigell's earlier induction even though he was Cabinet secretary at that time) but conveniently forgot his 2 August 1993 order freezing all elections and bye-elections till the Union government had met his demands on the disciplining of officers deemed on deputation with the Election Commission and the requirement of officers and police personnel during elections.

Dhanoa and Seigell and the Union Executive—despite Seshan as Cabinet secretary—had been amateurs. Dhanoa

*(1995) 4 SCC 611

and Seigell had walked into the Election Commission on the strength of Executive rules framed under Article 324(5) of the Constitution. Gill's and Krishnamurty's entry was professional. A presidential notification of 1 October 1993 fixed the strength of Election Commissioners at two. The same day another notification appointed Manohar Singh Gill and Gali Venkata Gopala Krishnamurty as election commissioners. That very day an ordinance putting the chief election commissioner and election commissioners at par in salary and allowances and fixing their term at six years, subject to the maximum age limit of sixty-five, was promulgated, which was called the Chief Election Commissioner and other Election Commissioners (Conditions of Service) Amendment Ordinance, 1993 and which sought to amend the 1991 Act differentiating between the chief election commissioner and the election commissioners. [It subsequently became the Chief Election Commissioner and other Election Commissioners (Conditions of Service) Amendment Act, 1994 without changes.] In other words Gill and Krishnamurty would be backed by parliamentary sanction.

Nevertheless Seshan decided not to recognize them, to the extent of denying them even sitting space in the commission. They gradually wore out the office, found a foothold as one would have done in an old-fashioned third-class railway carriage, and pressed much human flesh for their rights. But how were they to get down to doing official work when Seshan refused to engage them even in pleasantries, and the office staff showed them no papers?

That Seshan ignored them was reflected in his writ petition* before the Supreme Court. And in the preliminary

---

*(1995) 4 SCC 611

hearing by a division bench he seemed to have had everything his own way. On 15 November 1993 the court directed that:

> . . . until further orders, to ensure smooth and effective working of the Commission and also to avoid confusion both in the administration as well as in the electoral process, we direct that the Chief Election Commissioner shall remain in complete overall control of the Commission's work. He may ascertain the views of the other Commissioners or of such of them as he chooses, on the issues that may come up before the Commission from time to time. However, he will not be bound to their views. It is also made clear that the Chief Election Commissioner alone will be entitled to issue instructions to the Commission's staff as well as to the outside agencies and that no other Commissioner will issue such instructions.

Against all odds, Gill persisted with trying to work with his colleagues and to persuading Seshan that he had not come to wreck the commission but to help it arrive at rational and correct decisions. His behaviour was almost perfect. A shame GVG's Election Commission persona was associated with vituperation when in real life he is warm-hearted, witty and humorous. As for Seshan, he made full use of his untrammelled freedom under the preliminary direction of the Court—even when he went on leave, he put the office in charge of Deputy Election Commissioner D.S. Bagga, an IAS officer of joint secretary's rank on deputation with the commission. The Supreme Court in its final order directed that Gill would be in charge.

It was not the division bench any longer that was dealing with the case but a Constitution Bench (A.M. Ahmadi, CJI, J.S. Verma, N.P. Singh, S.P. Barucha and M.K. Mukherjee, JJ). In a unanimous decision* of 14 July 1995, the Constitution Bench not only dismissed Seshan's petition but disagreed with the main observations of the division bench in Dhanoa's case.†

It said:

That the Election Commission could either be a single member or multi-member body. It was not acceptable that a multi-member Commission was unworkable as this could be going against clauses (2) and (3) of Article 324; that the Commission discharged a public function and all the Commissioners had to contribute to decision-making. If the Chief Election Commissioner was considered superior to his colleagues, he would render them non-functional. The Election Commissioners were not there just to tender advice. The Chief Election Commissioner was not superior to his colleagues just because of the proviso to Article 324(5) which said that his conditions of service could not be varied to his disadvantage after appointment, whereas this was not extended to the Election Commissioners. Nor was he superior because he could be removed from office only by impeachment, and the other two on his recommendation. That the Election Commissioners could be removed on the recommendation of the Chief Election Commissioner

---

*(1995) 4 SCC 611
†AIR 1991 SC 1745

did not make them subordinate to him but only ensured their independence of the political Executive. The Chief Election Commissioner, in any case, could not recommend their removal out of whim or caprice and had to exercise his power with reason and responsibility. Article 324 envisaged the Election Commission as a permanent body headed by a permanent incumbent viz. the Chief Election Commissioner. He had to be treated differently if he had to maintain his independence. The Election Commissioners, on the other hand, were not intended to be permanent incumbents. In a multi-member body the Chief Election Commissioner was obliged to act as Chairman, to preside in meetings, preserve order, conduct the day's business, ensure precision of decisions taken, and see that they were correctly recorded. He had to ensure the smooth transaction of business; Parliament had the power to provide for the transaction of business of the Election Commission [the Chief Election Commissioner and other Election Commissioners (Conditions of Service) Amendment Act, 1994 had provided that all three Commissioners would have equal powers in decision-making, and that in the event of differences, the matter in hand would be decided by the majority] under clause (2) and (5) of Article 324, Articles 327 and 328 and Entry 72 of List (1) of the Seventh Schedule to the Constitution. There was no basis for the allegation of malafide against the Govt.

There was also a consequence of the Union Government's not having had the chief election commissioner as an independent constitutional authority in high office—as intended by the Constituent Assembly—but actually having brought him up in such a way that when he finally asserted himself he looked like an upstart. And no one likes an 'arriviste' in any official hierarchy. The court's observations were:

> In the instant case some of the service conditions of the CEC are akin to those of the Supreme Court Judges, namely, (i) the provision that he can be removed from office in like manner and on like grounds as a Judge of the Supreme Court and (ii) his conditions of service shall not be varied to his disadvantage after appointment. So far as the first is concerned instead of repeating the provisions of Article 124(4), the draftsman has incorporated the same by reference. The second provision is similar to the proviso to Article 125(2). But that does not confer the status of a Supreme Court Judge on the CEC. Of late it is found that even personnel belonging to other fora claim equation with High Court and Supreme Court Judges merely because certain jurisdictions earlier exercised by those Courts are transferred to them not realising the distinction between constitutional and statutory functionaries. The Government should not confer equivalence or interfere with the Warrant of Precedence, if it is likely to affect the position of High Court and Supreme Court Judges, however pressing the demand may be, without first seeking the views of the Chief Justice of India.

12

EC Frustrates Its Packers and Also More Than Earns Its Keep

The multi-member commission, the first time defenestrated and the second time tentative, became a reality when formally sanctioned by the Supreme Court. And it was a traumatic change from internal autocracy to oligarchy. In fact Seshan was so stunned by the court order and the whingeing observations against him that he was literally put out of action for the rest of his term. So the commission was run by the two election commissioners. This necessitated rude changes in the matrix of alliances and loyalties among the officers and staff of the Election Commission. The working methods became more friendly and decisions were not shoved down from the top but openly discussed.

But the court had made it clear that the multi-member commission was a temporary arrangement, implying that the Executive, if and when it so desired, could go back to a single-member body—as it did earlier. Obviously the Executive would not ordinarily do so arbitrarily. Nevertheless the institution had acquired an unenviable record for puerile and discordant inaction, and this had to be removed. With Seshan on the sidelines the Election Commission would have been a headless organization but for the Court's appreciating Gill's positive role and literally anointing him as the next chief election commissioner long before he became one.

Having got over its disabilities the multi-member commission had to perform and prove it was steadier and more objective than the one-man show. The consultative approach meant there were no more changes in the dates of elections and bye-elections because some important factors had been overlooked. The erratic manner in which bye-elections were held—in some cases after a vacancy of four to five years—ended. Every vacancy was filled within six months and the commission got the government to change the law to make this a requirement.

With Seshan's retirement, the confidence and authority of a cohesive three-member commission made it possible for an irretractable shift to electronic voting machines and an insistence on the identification of voters with identity cards. And the process of computerization of electoral rolls was completed. Most of all, closer attention to cleaning the electoral rolls and a more professional relationship with the home ministry and Department of Personnel in relation to officers and paramilitary forces required for election duty made for freer and fairer elections. A docile office staff ill-treated, then turned contumacious, then overindulged and become aggressive and opportunistic was slowly urged back to discipline. By the time the Gujarat assembly elections of 2002 arrived the multi-member commission had become, if anything, too independent for the government of the day and there were inspired leaks from time to time that it would become a five-member body.

But the multi-member commission is equally known for its many initiatives. The enforcement of internal democracy in political parties and of the law on disqualification of candidates and disclosures by candidates as well as the commission's contributions to time-sharing on radio and TV and upgradation of technology are hereafter dealt with in separate chapters.

{13}

Internal Democracy in
Political Parties

The Election Commission's exerting its authority vis-à-vis the Union government generally and the parties in power during elections have been dealt with. But for the last decade or so the commission has also been insisting that political parties be not only constituted democratically but also function thus.

I have referred to the remissness of the Constitution as well as the Representation of the People Acts, 1950 and 1951 with regard to their recognition of the existence of political parties despite the fact that everybody knew that parliamentary democracy was the chosen polity and that since the framing of the Constitution, elections and political parties had decided the governments of the day. The Election Commission, however, could not afford the luxury of ignoring political parties which it had to implicitly accept as legitimate electoral players from the very beginning. It provided for the registration of political parties, in the Election Symbols (Reservation and Allotment) Order, 1968. Registration with the Election Commission was a condition precedent for the recognition of a political party. It was not that an unregistered association of Indian citizens was debarred from contesting in an election; however, their candidate would be considered an independent.

It was only in 1989 that Parliament considered the registration of political parties important enough to come within the ambit of its own legislation. Part IVA was added to the Representation of the People Act, 1951 by an amendment which was to come into force on 15 June 1989. A new section, 29A, was introduced specifically for registering political parties. It sanctioned the arrangement under the Election Symbols (Reservation and Allotment) Order, 1968. However, there was an added perspective to the legislation as appeared in the Statement of Objects and Reasons to the bill which became the 1988 Act:

> . . . It is also felt that the political parties should be required to include a specific provision in the memorandum or rules or regulations governing their functioning that they would fully be committed to and abide by the principles enshrined in the preamble to the Constitution.

Accordingly even political parties registered under the Symbols Order of 1968 were obliged to register themselves afresh under Section 29A of the 1951 Act. Such parties were required to amend their constitutions to include an express provision 'that they shall bear true faith and allegiance to the Constitution and to the principles of socialism, secularism and democracy' and 'uphold the sovereignty, unity and integrity of India'.

The Supreme Court in *S.R. Bommai and Others Vs. Union of India and Others* noted that 'secularism' had not been defined, presumably because it was not capable of precise definition. The same with 'socialism'.

The Socialist Unity Centre of India (SUCI) felt uneasy about the definition of socialism being left to the Election Commission, and challenged Section 29A in the Delhi High Court mainly on the ground of unreasonable restrictions on the fundamental right to freedom of speech and expression, as well as to form an association; besides, it was against the basic structure of the Constitution and put the decision of the Election Commission on what constituted socialism beyond judicial scrutiny. The court rejected the contentions, holding the restrictions as reasonable in the interests of the sovereignty and integrity of India. The court also observed that principles of socialism, secularism and democracy were essential attributes of 'political morality' within the framework of the Indian Constitution. In the appeal the Supreme Court did not address the questions raised as the Union government and Parliament seemed to be contemplating further amendments to Section 29A. So the SUCI tidied up its constitution and got itself registered with the Election Commission.

The Punjab and Haryana High court in *Gurtej Singh Vs. Union of India and Others* very forthrightly held that if a candidate has to make an oath or affirmation to bear true faith and allegiance to the Constitution a similar requirement of a political party cannot be considered unconstitutional.

The courts having wisely steered clear from filling in for legislators and defining socialism and secularism, the Election Commission prudently concentrated on enforcing the political parties' allegiance to the principles of democracy. In Dispute Case No. 1 of 1994 regarding the Janata Dal, the Election Commission elaborated the concept in terms of lack of inner party democracy in political parties and 'non-holding of organisational elections at periodic intervals as provided for in the Constitution' as well as 'the negation of the right of participation to the primary members in the decision-making of the party and depriving them of their right of effective say in the running of the party's affairs'.

The Election Commission would not countenance this state of affairs, especially where national or state parties were involved. This was because they had special privileges like two free copies of the electoral roll at the stage of draft publication as well as after final publication, free time on All India Radio and Doordarshan during elections, exclusive allotment of reserved symbols, and preference in seating arrangements for their polling and counting agents in polling stations and counting halls. The political parties therefore were to constitute governing bodies/committees and elect office-bearers in accordance with their party constitutions within four months of the date of the order, that is, 16 October 1994. In any dispute as to which was the recognized party, where this was disputed by rival groups, and the matter was referred to the commission under para 15 of the symbols order, the result could be a declaration that none of the rival groups was the recognized party if the organizational elections had not been held according to the party constitution and the affairs of the party were being run in an ad hoc manner, and ad hoc arrangements were the general rule.

The order had little effect. Just before the 1996 parliamentary elections a petition was filed by Arjun Singh—claiming to be president of the Indian National Congress—under para 15 of the symbols order and praying for a declaration that the group headed by N.D. Tiwari was the real Indian National Congress and not the one under P.V. Narasimha Rao. Gill and Krishnamurty in their majority judgement inter alia referred to the Election Commission's

1994 order, noted that it had generally not been complied with by the political parties and therefore made no exception with the Narasimha Rao group which was effectively running the Indian National Congress. In effect this ruling group in the Indian National Congress, as well as the other parties, were given another opportunity to comply. Seshan, in his minority judgement, thought the 1994 orders were specific enough and ought to be implemented straightaway. Gill's and Krishnamurty's order meant the Indian National Congress was in the hands of Narasimha Rao's group, whereas Seshan's meant that none of the groups would be recognized.

What is significant is that parties heeded the instructions after 1996. Even the Shiv Sena which had Bal Thackeray as its 'sarsanchalak' or supreme leader for life, and had vested all the powers of the party in him, had to amend its constitution to make it a democratic party. An exception was the Indian National Congress which had not had any organizational elections the way that its constitution required for nearly twenty years. The commission threatened to cease correspondence with its office-bearers and thereby got it to comply.

14

Disqualification of Candidates

The prestige of the Election Commission has also been enhanced by tighter enforcement of the law on disqualification of convicted persons for candidature in elections to Parliament and the state legislatures. The convictions relate to electoral, economic and criminal offences. And the underlying assumption is that lawbreakers cannot be lawmakers.

The offences are of three categories depending on their nature and gravity and what effect they are likely to have on lawmakers and are stipulated in Section 8 of the Representation of the People Act, 1951:

- The first where mere conviction means disqualification for the period of sentence, if any, plus six years from the date of release.

- The second where the conviction results in a sentence of imprisonment for not less than six months. The disqualification is for the period of sentence of imprisonment and for another six years from the date of the release of the person sentenced.

- The third is where the accused is convicted and sentenced to imprisonment for not less than two years.

The disqualification is for the period of sentence of imprisonment and for a further period of six years from the date of release.

In all cases the disqualification applies from the date of conviction.

Offences of the first kind are mentioned in Section 8(1) of the Representation of the People Act, 1951. Examples are offences relating to enmity between different groups of people on grounds of religion, etc. (Section 153A), undue influence or personation in an election (Section 171F of IPC), rape (Sections 376 or 376A or 376B or 376C or 376D of IPC), the Foreign Exchange (Regulation) Act, 1973, the Narcotic Drugs and Psychotropic Substances Act, 1985 and insulting the national flag or the Constitution of India (Section 2 of the Prevention of Insults to National Honour Act, 1971).

Examples of the second kind—in Section 8(2) of the 1951 Act—are contraventions of the laws on the prevention of hoarding or profiteering and the adulteration of food or drugs and of the Dowry Prohibition Act, 1961.

The third category is of offences other than those in the first two categories under which the accused is convicted and sentenced to imprisonment for not less than two years.

However, the disqualifications in Section 8(1), Section 8(2) and Section 8(3) do not apply to a person who, on the date of his conviction, is a sitting member of Parliament or of a state legislature. Section 8(4) says that disqualification of such a member will not take effect until three months from the date of conviction. Even this has a qualification for if within three months he prefers an appeal or revision petition with respect to such conviction or sentence, the disqualification will not come into effect until the petition is disposed of by the higher court. What is to be noted is that he continues to get the benefit of this provision even if he ceases to be a member of Parliament or a state legislature in the meantime.

Though Section 8 unambiguously stipulates that the disqualification will be attracted by the convicted person from the date of his conviction, there was a general understanding, though erroneous, that the conviction meant final conviction by the court of appeal or revision where an appeal or application for revision was filed and pending and not by the trial court. (Convicted persons often became candidates at elections if they were released on bail pending the disposal of their appeal or application for revision.) This understanding of the law was accepted by everyone till August 1997 when the commission, after making a close examination of several judgements of the high courts of Allahabad, Mumbai, Madhya Pradesh, Himachal Pradesh and of the Supreme Court corrected that impression and brought out the true intent of Section 8. The commission issued an order on 28 August 1997 clarifying the legal position that a person incurred disqualification under Section 8 right from the date of conviction by the trial court and the grant of bail to the convict by the appellate or revisionary court had no effect on his disqualification—he continued to suffer from that disqualification even if he was released on bail during the pendency of his appeal or revision application. Some doubts were expressed in certain legal circles about the clarification so given by the commission, but these were set at rest by the judgement of the Supreme Court in the case of *Km. Jayalalitha* on 21 September 2001. The apex court found her disqualified for election to the Tamil Nadu legislative assembly despite the fact that she was freed on bail during the pendency of her appeal before the high court as she stood, at that time, convicted by a criminal court in a land deal case and sentenced to imprisonment for three years.

In order to give teeth to its clarification, the commission also prescribed an affidavit—GVG's initiative—to be filed by all candidates giving the details of their convictions, if any, under Section 8. The Supreme Court held in the case of *Shaligram Srivastava* that non-filing of the above affidavit by any candidate could be a ground for rejection of the nomination.

15

Disclosures by Candidates

In the middle of 2002 the Election Commission's stature in the eye of the public so leapt upwards it seemed to be in active alliance with the voter and the court against the corrupt political class.

Over a period of time recommendations for political reform had accumulated without the slightest response from the Union government. The main ones dealt with counting the expenses of party, friends and relatives in the expenditure of the candidate, disallowing defections and shutting out criminals from electoral competition. The Election Commission, Goswami Committee Report (1990), Law Commission Report (1999), and National Commission to Review the Working of the Constitution Report (2002) had stressed on these.

With politics getting murkier and governments becoming more meaningless on the one hand, and politicians being uninterested in electoral reforms on the other, the middle-class voter decided to go to court to secure an order requiring more transparency about the antecedents of candidates. (The Indian urban middle class, like anywhere else, assumes the electorate will harshly repel a candidate with a criminal record. It also believes in accountability—

that election results reflect the performance or non-performance of the government of the day. The rural majority is more impressed with raw power and patronage/destructive potential.) That is, the middle-class voter as represented by the Association for Democratic Reforms—academics from Ahmedabad and Hyderabad so highly motivated as to pay for the expenses out of their own pocket.

The Delhi High Court, in its order of 2 November 2000, held that to enable the voter to make the right choice it was necessary that he know the past of a candidate. The Election Commission was directed to secure to the voter the following information on candidates contesting Parliament and state legislature elections: offences punishable with imprisonment of which a candidate is accused; assets possessed by a candidate, his or her spouse and dependent relations; facts giving an insight into a candidate's competence, capacity and suitability for being a parliamentarian or legislator including his/her educational qualifications; information which the Election Commission considers necessary for judging the capacity and capability of the political party fielding the candidate for election to Parliament or the state legislature.

The Union of India, in an appeal before the Supreme Court, asserted that the high court ought to have directed the petitioners to Parliament to seek amendments to the law, instead of issuing a directive to the Election Commission. The Supreme Court in its order of 2 May 2002* *Union of India Vs. Association for Democratic Reforms and Others* held that:

People's Union for Civil Liberties Vs. Union of India and Others, (2003) 4 SCC 399 the jurisdiction of the Election Commission is comprehensive enough to include all powers necessary for the smooth conduct of elections;

there is a limitation to its plenary powers by way of specific provisions of the law made by Parliament or a State Legislature; where the law is silent, the Commission has to exercise its residuary powers especially in the context of an infinite variety of situations, unforeseen contingencies not anticipated by the law. The Commission is perfectly competent to issue directions till the vacuum is filled by legislation [italics mine];

fair elections require the candidate's disclosure of his past and of his assets. Power and black money are in symbiotic relationship. A voter can at least decide whether a candidate with black money can be re-elected;

in the interests of transparency and purity of the elections the Commission can ask the candidate how much expenditure has been incurred by the party on him;

the right to information is natural to a democracy. This is evident from Articles 19(1) and (2) of the International Covenant of Civil and Political Rights;

where the field meant for the Legislature and Executive is unoccupied, and this is detrimental to the public interest the court, under Article 32 read with Articles 141 and 142 of the Constitution, can issue directions to the Executive to subserve public interest;

Article 19(1)(a) of the Constitution provides for freedom of speech and expression. The voter's speech

or expression in an election includes his casting a
vote. So information on the candidate is absolutely
necessary.

[Accordingly] *the Election Commission is directed
to call for information on affidavit by issuing
necessary order in exercise of its power under Art.
324 of the Constitution of India from each candidate
seeking election to Parliament or a state legislature
as a necessary part of his nomination paper,
furnishing therein, information on the following
aspects in relation to his/her candidature* [italics mine]:

(1) Whether the candidate is convicted/acquitted/
discharged of any criminal offence in the past if any;
whether he is punished with imprisonment or fine?

(2) Prior to six months of filing of nomination,
whether the candidate is accused in any pending
case, of any offence punishable with imprisonment
for two years or more, and in which charge is
framed or cognizance is taken by the court of law.
If so, the details thereof.

(3) The assets (immovable, movable, bank balances
etc) of a candidate and of his/her spouse and that of
dependants.

(4) Liabilities, if any, particularly whether there are
any overdues of any public financial institution or
government dues.

(5) The educational qualifications of the candidate.

The Election Commission was given two months to give
effect to the directions of the court.

The commission considered that the best way to
implement the directions was to amend the nomination

forms and recommended this to the Ministry of Law. After reminders the ministry requested the commission to approach the Supreme Court for an additional two months time as the Union government proposed to discuss the matter with political parties. The commission told the ministry it was for the Union of India to approach the Court if it considered this necessary. Since the Court had not extended the time given for implementing its directions the Election Commission issued the following order on 28 June, 2002:

Every candidate, while filing his nomination paper shall furnish full and complete information on the points specified by the court in an affidavit;

The affidavit shall be sworn before a Magistrate or Notary Public or Commissioner of Oaths;

Not furnishing the affidavit shall be considered a violation of the Supreme Court's order and the nomination shall be liable to rejection;

Wrong or incomplete information or suppression of any material information, if considered a defect of substantial character, may also result in a rejection of the nomination paper;

Provided only such information shall be considered wrong or incomplete or amounting to suppression of material information as is capable of easy verification by the returning officer;

The information given by each candidate shall be disseminated by the returning officer by putting the affidavit on his notice board and making copies freely available to other candidates and the media;

Any information to the contrary from a rival candidate in a duly sworn affidavit shall also be so disseminated.

Every single political party was averse to what amounted to the candidates stripping in public and the result was the presidential promulgation of the Representation of the People (Amendment) Ordinance, 2002, of 24 August inserting Sections 33A, 33B and 125A as well as amending Section 169 of the Representation of the People Act, 1951.

Section 33B rendered the Election Commission order of 28 June ineffective as it read:

> 33B.Notwithstanding anything contained in any judgement, decree or order of any court or any direction, order or any other instruction issued by the Election Commission, no candidate shall be liable to disclose or furnish any such information, in respect of his election, which is not required to be disclosed or furnished under this Act or the rules made thereunder.

The Association for Democratic Reforms, People's Union for Civil Liberties and Lok Satta filed writ petitions before the Supreme Court against the Presidential ordinance.

The ordinance was substituted by the Representation of the People (Third Amendment) Act, 2002.

The petitioners filed applications saying their writ petitions should be treated as challenging the constitutional validity of the Representation of the People (Third Amendment) Act, 2002.

The Supreme Court, in its order of 13 March 2003, declared Section 33B of the amended Act illegal, null and void.

Justice P.V. Reddi's directions—concurred in by Justice D.M. Dharmadhikari—were:

> 6. The right to information provided for by the Parliament under Section 33A in regard to the

pending criminal cases and past involvement in such cases is reasonably adequate to safeguard the right to information vested in the voter/citizen. However, there is no good reason for excluding the pending cases in which cognizance has been taken by Court from the ambit of disclosure.

9. The Election Commission has to issue revised instructions to ensure implementation of Section 33A subject to what is laid down in this judgement regarding the cases in which cognizance has been taken. The Election Commission's orders related to disclosure of assets and liabilities will still hold good and continue to be operative. However, direction No. 4 of para 14 insofar as verification of assets and liabilities by means of summary enquiry and rejection of nomination paper on the ground of furnishing wrong information or suppressing material information should not be enforced.

Justice M.B. Shah, who agreed that Section 33B was illegal, null and void further directed:

It is true that the aforesaid directions issued by the Election Commission is not under challenge but at the same time prima facie it appears that the Election Commission is required to revise its instructions in the light of directions issued in Association for Democratic Reforms case (*supra*) and as provided under the Representation of the People Act and its 3rd Amendment.

The Election Commission accordingly amended its earlier order.

16

Time-sharing on Radio and TV

Again, at a time when 'state-funding' (of elections) was the buzz word and the Union government was quite inert, the Election Commission brought out and implemented a viable time-sharing scheme in respect of the use of government-owned radio and television by political parties at election time. That was in 1998.

In the middle of the last century it was the government-owned All India Radio, and later—when television was in vogue—the government-owned Doordarshan which provoked the ire of opposition parties, the point made being that the government in power had the unfair advantage of using these facilities against them at elections. The Congress ignored the criticism but the Janata government in 1977 was sensitive enough to it to formulate a maiden but nominal time-sharing scheme in parliamentary elections. A recognized national party was allowed two fifteen-minute broadcasts on the national station of All India Radio and one fifteen-minute telecast on the national channel of Doordarshan, as well as two broadcasts and one telecast from the principal stations of AIR and Doordarshan in all the states. A recognized state party could make two similar broadcasts and one telecast from the principal stations of

AIR and Doordarshan in the state concerned. In state assembly elections the facilities of two broadcasts and one telecast were applicable to each national party and each state party of the state concerned. The dates and timings were determined by lot. The scheme survived two writ petitions—one each in the Gujarat and Delhi high courts— saying the facilities were discriminating to independent candidates.

By 1998 the outreach of both AIR and Doordarshan was co-extensive with the extent of the country. Since the context was state-funding of political parties, what was needed was no longer token but substantial use of the facilities by the parties to really cut down their expenditure. This at a time when their expenditure, particularly on the electronic media, was running out of proportion to other expenditure. There was also a commendable neatness about such extended time-sharing. While the parties would be given time vouchers with implied money value worked out on the basis of the opportunity cost of the time allotted, no money passed into the hands of the political parties.

The scheme was discussed by the Election Commission with the national and state parties on 7 May 1997, and 22 and 23 December of the same year. And then with Prasar Bharati Corporation. The scheme as announced on 16 January 1998 is:

The above facility of use of Doordarshan (DD) and All India Radio (AIR) shall be available, in connection with the forthcoming general elections to the House of the People and the Legislative Assemblies of the States of Gujarat, Himachal Pradesh, Meghalaya, Nagaland and Tripura, only to those seven (7) National Parties and thirty-four (34) States Parties, which are at present recognized as such National or State Parties, under the provisions of the Election Symbols (Reservation and Allotment) Order 1968 . . . This facility will not be available to candidates.

The Supreme Court has held in the case of *Ramakant Pandey Vs. Union of India* that the recognized national and state parties stand on a different footing from the unrecognized political parties and any discrimination between these two categories of political parties would be a reasonable and valid classification. At present also, the above-mentioned limited facility of telecasts or broadcasts is available only to the recognized national and state parties. The high courts of Allahabad, Madras and Karnataka have also upheld the above classification in *Hari Shankar Jain Vs. Chief Election Commissioner and Ors., P.T. Srinivasan Vs. Union of India and Ors.* and *S. Shanmugam Vs. Chief Electoral Officer, Tamil Nadu and Ors.* and *Raghunathmal Vs. Election Commission of India and Ors.* respectively. The Madras High Court has, in these cases, specifically upheld the grant of facility of telecasts or broadcasts only to the recognized political parties.

In general elections to Parliament and the state legislatures the Prasar Bharati Corporation would set apart on Doordarshan:

(a) a total of not less than 10 hours of telecasting time on the National Channel of the Doordarshan, for telecasts by the National parties;

(b) a total of not less than 15 hours of telecasting time on the regional Doordarshan Kendras, for telecasts by the National parties;

(c) a total of not less than 30 hours of telecasting time on the regional Doordarshan Kendras, for telecasts by the State parties; and

(d) a total of 6 hours of telecasting time through the Regional Satellite Services channel available to viewers across the whole country.

On All India Radio

(e) a total of not less than 10 hours of broadcasting time on the National hookup of All India Radio for broadcasts by the National parties;

(f) a total of not less than 15 hours of broadcasting time on the regional AIR Stations for broadcasts by the National parties;

(g) a total of not less than 30 hours of broadcasting time on the regional AIR Stations, for broadcasts by the State parties;

(h) a total of 6 hours broadcasting time on the National hookup for broadcasts by the State parties.

The allocation of time to each national party would be determined by the parameters given below:

(a) of the total 10 hours telecasting/broadcasting time reserved over the National channel/hookup of DD/AIR for the National parties, 45 minutes shall be allotted to each of the 7 National parties, i.e., a total of 5-1/4 hours each on the DD and AIR separately;

(b) the remaining 4-3/4 hours telecasting/broadcasting time shall be further divided among the seven National parties, according to the percentage of votes polled by each such party, at the last general election to the House of the People held in 1996;

(c) in addition, each national party shall be allotted one and a half times of the total time allotted to it under sub-paras (a) and (b) above, for telecasts/broadcasts on the Regional Doordarshan Kendras/Regional AIR Stations;

(d) of the total time so allotted to each National party under sub-para(c), each such party shall have the option to utilise the time so allotted on any of the Regional Doordarshan Kendra/State capital AIR Station—provided that not more than one-tenth of such time shall be utilised by it at any one Regional Doordarshan Kendras/AIR Stations.

As between state parties the arrangement would be:

(e) of the total time of 30 hours reserved for telecasting/broadcasting by the State parties on the Regional DD Kendras/Regional AIR Stations, each of the 34 State parties shall be allotted 45 minutes, i.e., a total of 25-1/2 hours, each on DD and AIR separately;

(f) the remaining 4-1/2 hours telecasting/broadcasting time for parties shall be further divided among the said 34 State parties, according to the percentage of votes polled by each such party in the State(s) in which it is recognised, at the last general election to the House of the People held in 1996, and the last general election to the Legislative Assembly of the State concerned, taken together;

(g) in addition, each State party shall be allotted 10 minutes telecasting/broadcasting time on Regional Satellite Services channel of DD available to viewers across the whole country and the National hookup of AIR.

Again the actual slots were predetermined by lots.

17

Upgradation of Technology

Another feather was added to the Election Commission's cap when it became one of the most electronically advanced state institutions in the country. It had computerized electoral rolls, their off-shoot, electors' photo identity cards (EPICs), electronic voting machines and an extensive wide-area-network (WAN) linking each state and district to the commission.

From a modest platform of computers at commission headquarters and in the offices of chief electoral officers a comprehensive programme for computerization of electoral rolls for the entire country was launched in 1997. The programme required construction of a database for a 620 million-plus electorate in fourteen regional languages, besides English. The programme also required preparing and issuing EPICs using the database of the electoral rolls. Uniformity of the entire computerization effort was essential and for this a set of standardized guidelines incorporating forty-two inter-linked control tables for managing the relevant information of the electors was laid down.

For over five years—since 1997—the entire country has had a computerized database of 620 million-plus electors arranged on a household basis and aggregated polling station-wise and then assembly constituency-wise. The annual revision done either summarily or intensively has enabled the commission to remove the errors and discrepancies that creep into the database.

Computer internet technology was additionally integrated into the work of the commission with the launching of the official website, *www.eci.gov.in* in January, 1998. The wide area network (WAN) was established with chief electoral officers of sixteen states over leased lines and these were integrated to district centres at the time of elections. By the General Elections to Parliament in 1999, direct links had been set up with 1,200 counting centres to capture round-wise trends and results and these, in turn, were posted in real time on the website. At the time, this was one of the most extensive WANs in the country—with state-of-the-art technology.

The EC website tried to give the trends and results well ahead of the other agencies including the media. (There was a ban on sharing this data with the National Informatic Centre—an organization that used to provide data to various news channels through district networks.) But accuracy has a price. The Election Commission could not compete with the news channels, which could give trends on the basis of telephonic messages or even hearsay. The expectations of netizens was so high that the EC website recorded several million hits on counting day. This choked the system and rendered access impossible at times.

The practice of reporting round-wise counting trends was discontinued in 2001. The reason was the extensive use of electronic voting machines, which gave instant results and reduced counting time to nothing.

The transition from the Balloting System to the Marking System and introduction of the electronic voting machine have been alluded to. Since 2002, the commission had decided that elections would in future be only by the EVM and had ensured that the procurement and disposition of machines followed the pattern.

Widening the use of technology included plotting electoral rolls on the website as well as instructions on Voice Over Internet Protocol (VOIP).

18

EC in Jammu and Kashmir

Nevertheless, the reputation of the Election Commission in Jammu and Kashmir in September 2002, was unenviable. Much of it was a matter of tradition, the state, if various press reports and other accounts are to believed, evidently having been a pioneer in mass rigging. According to the *Kashmir Times* of 18 June 2002—under the caption: 'More than Fair'—in the 1951 elections to the state constituent assembly conducted under the state's own dispensation, Sheikh Abdullah, as state prime minister, ensured that all the National Conference candidates were elected unopposed. Most of the nomination papers of the opposition were rejected, and where this did not happen, opposition candidates were either abducted or forced to withdraw. Shamim Ahmed Shamim's pejorative for the Congress legislators elected in 1967 was 'Khaliq-made MLAs'. They were named after Abdul Khaliq Malik, the deputy commissioner of Anantnag at the time. In this context it was the Congress candidates who were declared unopposed while the nominations of the others were rejected.

An example of rigging in the 1987 elections has been given in an earlier chapter. There are many more pre-poll, poll and post-poll irregularities mentioned in the *India*

Today issue of 15 April 1987: six hundred workers of the opposition were arrested in Muslim United Front (MUF), independents and People's Conference (PC)-dominated areas; voters were not allowed to vote in Kawari and 250 potential Abdul Gani Lone voters were physically ejected from a polling booth area by National Conference (NC) activists. In Pattan, ballot books allegedly already stamped for the NC were recovered by opposition parties. In Khansahib and Hazratbal, NC partymen in Matadors reportedly drove to the polling stations and entered the booths doing what they liked. With the National Conference and Congress already certain of victory, MUF leaders were being arrested and slapped with charges of anti-national activities. Anantnag, Sopore, Handwara and Baramulla were in some kind of curfew while results were being tabulated. In Kupwara and Handwara districts, where Lone held sway, counting in many polling booths was postponed. When it began on 26 March, Lone and his counting agents were expelled from the counting station. Lone had complained officially that some 100 boxes had been removed at night from the counting station and a hundred of his agents had been arrested. Two days later, he was declared to have lost by 1,300 votes; one of the counting stations was an agricultural college near Sopore. A traffic jam in driving rain was alleged to have been manipulated to stop and unload buses carrying ballot boxes, two kilometres before the counting station, presumably so that the boxes could be switched. There were examples of polling officers not sealing boxes on the pretext that they had no seals.

Farooq's election results were declared in three hours while the results of Anantnag district were declared after two-and-a-half days. Counting officers in Anantnag, some of whom were illiterate forest guards, stopped whenever they found an opposition candidate was leading. When the MUF candidate Sayed Shah was declared elected, agents of the opposing parties took ballot papers out of their boxes and the presiding officer in the counting hall stopped further proceedings. In another case, counting was suspended when an MUF candidate took an early lead. In the counting hall in Dooru, with one ballot box of 1,100 votes still to be counted, an NC candidate with a lead of 300 votes was declared winner.

After the 1987 elections militancy and anti-militancy operations took over. In the elections after 1989 while Pakistan and its agents threatened potential voters with death, the security forces in places seem to have countered by coercing people to vote, though in all fairness not telling them whom or which party to vote for. The Election Commission, at these elections, always appeared to be in the company of, and therefore in collaboration with, security forces and partisan state government functionaries through whom the elections had had to be conducted.

There were other reasons why the chief electoral officer of the state—the Election Commission's representative—had made no impact on the elections. The elections had always been remote-controlled, hands-off events for the Election Commission, even before militancy began. It was almost as if (and I too was part of this dispensation) the commission implicitly believed that the home ministry and security forces knew best how to run the state, and through whom, and the elections were best left to take their own course. All that was needed was for somebody from the Election Commission to make a token appearance in the state before voting, preferably by helicopter.

The Model Code of Conduct, the most effective equalizer of candidates and political parties, but which bit into Indian elections only in the early 1990s, had never been enforced in Jammu and Kashmir. There are some apparently outrageous examples of violation of the Model Code on which the Election Commission turned its back:

In the *Tribune* of 8 March 1987 Farooq Abdullah, at his public meetings in Batote, Ramban and Banihal, is reported to have announced ten micro-hydel projects on the Chenab. This was just about two weeks before the elections; again on 26 February, according to the *Tribune* of 27 February 1987, the Union minister of state for civil supplies, Ghulam Nabi Azad, had announced five new godowns, each with a capacity of 5,000 tons, for the district towns of Doda, Kupwara, Leh, Poonch and Rajouri.

The one single election which was supposed to be a good election—of 1977—was attributed entirely to Prime Minister Morarji Desai. He promised fair elections and was as good as his word. But what is equally important is that since Morarji was neither associated with the Congress nor the National Conference but was heading a mere Janata government, he was more credible to the common Kashmiri. The Election Commission, as far as the people were concerned, might never have existed. And if it did, as a substitute for the earlier dispensation and therefore an extension of the long hand of India into Kashmir, it could never be fully trusted in any case.

Part Two

A Necessary Progression

Ultimately, the worth of the Election Commission had to be reflected in better elections. The Kashmir elections as they turned out would have been impossible but for the upping of the quality of such exercises by the use of identity cards and EVMs across the board from 2001, and still more, by close and persistent attention to the correctness of the electoral rolls—though 2001 presented some problems—from 2002. Not that this later development came on its own. It was compelled by two sets of circumstances, one internal and concerning gross manipulation of the electoral rolls—to be related later—and another external, the Election Commission's experience of the Australian general elections of 2001.

Deputy Election Commissioners Sayan Chatterjee, Ajay Narayan Jha and I were at the Australian general elections in November 2001. Though the number of voters was just 12 million in a population of 18 million, the accuracy of the electoral rolls—including the addresses—was such that if by noon someone had not voted, the Australian Election Commission would ask by e-mail or otherwise why they had not done so, voting in Australia being compulsory. We were thoroughly impressed and came back determined to work towards similar electoral rolls in India, though aware that the Australian context was much more relaxed. By way of diversion here is an extract from my tour note:

> The 10th was election day and we were at a polling station in Boddington Crescent Primary School. Party representatives, with their handouts, were already waylaying voters outside. And the limited poster-space had been taken by first-comers. In the land of compulsory voting, the entire household turns up at the polling station—dogs, babies, old folks you'd think would disintegrate with exposure. It's the only social event in which the whole country is engaged— a reversion to tribalism in that sense. (Some of the dogs tied outside were spoiling for a fight. All kinds of dogs but no kelpi, a smallish, indigenous shepherd dog with a reputation for manipulating sheep as well as humans. What would a kelpi do if attacked by a dingo or Australian wild dog, I asked Mark Durr. The reply—if there were too many dingoes, the kelpi would probably run to the police station for help. Just a sample of the Australian humour you'll find everywhere.)

Elections in 2001 were in Tamil Nadu, Kerala, West Bengal, Pondicherry and Assam. Except for Assam, EVMs and identity cards were used everywhere.

In Tamil Nadu, J. Jayalalitha of the AIADMK, then in the opposition, virulently held forth against the use of EVMs and filed a writ petition in the Madras High Court. The high court upheld the commission's directions and when its orders were challenged, the Supreme Court came to the same conclusion. Nevertheless, the AIADMK won the elections handsomely.

The Congress in Kerala alleged widespread stuffing of the panchayat rolls with under-aged persons and a corresponding deletion of the names of Congress supporters. Panchayat elections preceded the assembly elections. The point was to find a prophylactic for the Parliament and assembly electoral rolls which were then being revised. An inquiry team suggested the following correctives:

(i) Strict verification of new claims particularly of those who were attaining the age of 18 for the first time and entering the electoral rolls. Since Kerala is a highly literate State, school leaving certificates were insisted upon to verify the age;

(ii) proper verification of dead electors through death registers which again were properly maintained in the State;

(iii) adopting a transparent approach in disposal of claims and objections and decentralisation of verification procedure;

(iv) photographing of new electors whose claims were provisionally accepted simultaneously with scrutinising their applications to ensure that the right persons came for enrolment (identity cards were issued only after final publication of the rolls.)

The Left Front government lost the elections.

Though the West Bengal election results fairly accurately mirrored the respective strengths of the parties in the fray, they were somewhat sullied by protracted negative publicity on the alleged systematic purging of Trinamool Congress supporters in parts of Midnapore district and complaints of partisanship against state government officials who had become too friendly and comfortable with the CPM, which had ruled continuously for twenty-six years and seemed as inevitable as the rising sun. The CPM retained West Bengal.

The elections in Pondicherry were efficient and relatively quiet. The ruling Dravida Munnetra Kazhagam (DMK)– Tamil Manila Congress (TMC) alliance lost the elections, the Indian National Congress (INC) won. In Assam, the Congress came back to power.

The first tranche of elections in 2002 included Uttar Pradesh, Uttaranchal, Punjab and Manipur. Apart from Manipur (EVMs were used in six assembly constituencies. At one time the ID cards had covered 75 per cent of the electors. Thereafter, the programme was discontinued when ID cards were burnt by the underground in the hill areas) identity cards and EVMs were used without exception. But it was realized that the electoral roll and its annual revision was a serious and recurring problem—in fact the main problem—which every chief electoral officer in every state and his successor would not only have to live with but satisfactorily tackle every year.

In Uttar Pradesh there were complaints about the electoral rolls of Thakurdwara, Pratapgarh, Ayodhya and Varanasi. Thakurdwara was a traumatic experience for the Election Commission as an inquiry revealed 15,800 Muslim voters had been deliberately left out while 21,000 non-existent but apparently Hindu voters were added. The officer who was district magistrate when the electoral rolls were revised and other officers were suspended. The rolls were rectified and the ruling BJP not only lost the elections but trailed the Samajwadi and Bahujan Samajwadi parties.

Conditions in Punjab were equally reprehensible. There were complaints of defects in the electoral rolls of Amritsar, Kapurthala and Faridkot districts. An inquiry indicated that in 23-Tarn Taran, 25-Naushera Panwan and 40-Bholath assembly constituencies bulk applications for inclusion of names in the electoral roll were received by the electoral registration officers; no individual orders were passed even though the electoral registration officers were supposed to do so; many blank forms were accepted without proper signatures.

The SDMs of Tarn Taran and Bholath and an executive magistrate of Tarn Taran were suspended and the deputy commissioners of Amritsar and Kapurthala were transferred.

The Congress in Punjab was as hysterically opposed to EVMs as the AIADMK in Tamil Nadu and approached the Punjab and Haryana High Court. The court did not allow the Congress petition but directed the commission to hear the petitioners on their objections. The Congress had alleged that the Shiromani Akali Dal, the ruling party, had manipulated the EVMs in stock with the Punjab government and so had won some elections where the Congress predominated. All that was needed was to substitute one electronic chip for another, and the Congress said they had been able to demonstrate this in their prototype machine. Given an opportunity in the Election Commission they failed to prove that the commission's machine could be tampered with the way they said their own machine could. All the same the commission substituted the Punjab machines with another set and observers were placed in advance to monitor the receipt and storage of the replacement EVMs as well as to oversee the pre-poll preparation of the machines and their post-poll storage. As in Tamil Nadu the ruling party lost.

In the Uttaranchal elections the ruling BJP lost.

In Manipur—the volatile state which was largely outside the writ of the government and too thinly covered by security forces—elections of a sort were held with some violence and the ruling People's Front was toppled.

Simultaneously, there were bye-elections to the Jammu Lok Sabha constituency. These were mired in controversy. The counting process was boycotted midway by the opposition parties who asserted that extensive rigging and booth-capturing had occurred. The commission allowed the counting to continue but stipulated that the results not be declared till it gave the nod. The observers and the deputy commissioner, Jammu—also returning officer—were summoned and questioned. The records were also examined. It was seen that in the higher reaches of Poonch and Rajouri sectors where logistic constraints did not allow close supervision, an exceptionally high percentage of voting in some polling stations had been registered. Since the difference between the leading candidate and the next was such that even if the re-poll of the questionable polling stations took place it would not affect the final result, the Commission issued a statement stating that 'there being no compelling reason to intervene, the results of the polls for Jammu Parliamentary Constituency may be declared'. What is important is that this bye-election was a timely warning of the kind of malpractices that could occur in the approaching Jammu and Kashmir assembly elections, particularly in pockets combining logistic and militancy problems.

Part Three

Before March 2002—
Nothing Much

The Jammu and Kashmir elections, for the Election Commission, did not begin with the announcement and end with the counting, as most elections do. It was a complex spider's web including threads a year before and after. One can only attempt to recall the strands chronologically, that being the only way the elections can be understood.

The then chief electoral officer of Uttar Pradesh, Noor Mohammad, remembers me having shown concern about how to computerize the Jammu and Kashmir electoral rolls in Urdu as early as May 2001 on the return journey from Gaumukh, a high-altitude pilgrimage destination now in the new state of Uttaranchal. Apparently I had asked him to accompany Shailendra Mendiratta, a computer-savvy deputy election commissioner, to the Centre for Development of Advanced Computing, Pune, which had been tasked to design software for data entry in the Nastalik script of Urdu—the one used in Kashmir. A phone call from Mendiratta to Noor Mohammad and the communication between the two ended.

At the end of an August 2001 tour to Buddhist Leh,

Muslim Kargil and Buddhist Padum, in which one was able to appreciate the unhealthy electoral rivalry between Leh and Kargil—including unrestrained breeding—districts that shared a member of Parliament. Chief Minister Farooq Abdullah invited me to dinner in Srinagar on 25 August. But that evening he had to go to Jammu where militants had struck again. One was able, however, to convince Mushtaq Ahmad Lone, minister of law, about the need for identity cards, electronic voting machines and computerization of electoral rolls in the state. During the day I had met my old friend Tony Jaitley, the chief secretary, who was recuperating at home. He too was very receptive.

On 5 September I chaséd this with a letter to the chief minister saying that the Jammu and Kashmir electoral law had to be amended to provide for the use of EVMs. Despite the amendment's having to be passed by both Houses of the state legislature and the upper House being partially gutted in a bomb attack, a prompt, pleasant and positive reply came with a letter dated 16 October. The law had been amended and EVMs, identity cards and computerization of rolls were welcomed with the condition that the commission find the funds for an identity card programme, which would be expensive.

On 23 November 2001 Mufti Muhammad Sayeed of the Peoples Democratic Party saw me and wanted an intensive revision of the electoral rolls in preparation for the 2002 Jammu and Kashmir assembly poll. He indicated that the rolls had been last intensively revised in 1988 and summarily revised subsequently. So there was a mother roll with innumerable supplementary ones. These rolls carried a lot of dead and shifted voters. Besides, summary revision required potential voters to visit electoral registration officers to file applications for inclusion in the electoral roll, which for fear of militants, they were not prepared to do. So there ought to be intensive revision in 2002. My reply was: It was even more inconceivable in the prevailing violence and insecurity in the state that the humble enumerator (usually a schoolteacher unwillingly drafted for the work and very poorly paid for it) would go from door to door, enrolling voters; in the event of an intensive revision, opposition parties would level the charge that the ruling party had misused state machinery and, under cover of abnormal circumstances in the state, quietly removed their supporters from the rolls, substituting them with its own; militants (militancy grew apace in 1989, that is, after the 1988 intensive revision) could organize protests by individuals saying they were not Indians and would not get themselves enrolled; so the summary revision should continue.

'*But Kashmir is different,*' he said, and instead of addressing the ground situation suggested we were shirking our responsibility in not doing intensive revision. He was then reminded that it was the responsibility of political parties to ensure that intending voters submitted applications in Form 6, and other knowledgeable people put in applications in Form 7 for the deletion of dead voters. Why didn't his party fan out into the field for the purpose? It was not the most friendly encounter.

One was not happy about the manipulation of the electoral rolls in the run up to the Punjab elections and in the midst of those elections in February 2002 a technical committee said it would take at least a year to computerize the Jammu and Kashmir rolls. So one wanted Deputy Election Commissioner Sayan Chatterjee to take charge of both Punjab and Jammu and Kashmir from Shailendra. But there was a delay in Director Ajay Jha's promotion and the re-distribution of states between the deputy election commissioners. Shailendra completed the Punjab elections and kept Jammu and Kashmir with him till 4 April 2002. Fortunately Sayan was consulted in everything that mattered and from February onwards he was the key figure in the state's affairs.

My friend and batchmate in the Indian Administrative Service Moni Malhoutra, once assistant secretary general in the Commonwealth Secretariat, rang me on 30 January wanting to know if we were going to have 'international observers' in Kashmir. I requested him to drop in, which he did, but unfortunately just before one of our commission meetings. So people filtered into my room and rather hurriedly knocked the idea out of shape in no time at all, much to Moni's irritation.

Discussing the Jammu and Kashmir elections with me in February, Sayan was still in the old comfortable, remote-control groove and smiled unbelievingly—Sayan, then the tallest member of the IAS, was used to reducing people to their basic chemistry and was naturally sceptical about things—when told we would do a thorough hands-on operation for a change and visit the state as many times as was needed. Was I serious or just being flippant? How could one not be serious, he was made to see, when the Indian middle class and the international community, as never before, were expectantly and uncompromisingly waiting for clean elections. With the reputation of the Election Commission at stake we obviously could not afford to leave everything to the chief electoral officer of Jammu and Kashmir, and the sooner we took on board the necessary physical courage and commitment to the job the better. Sayan had already emphathized with me before I had finished. He soon showed Noor a sample of the Jammu and Kashmir electoral rolls in Urdu and wanted to know if there was a way to computerize them. Noor, a maths wizard from a pathshala in Basti, began to ponder the problem.

March to Mid-June 2002—Handling Demands of Political Parties and Laying Down Policies

The commission's—my colleague Brij Behari Tandon, Sayan Chatterjee, Shailendra Mendiratta and I were in the team—first trip to the state was on 8 and 9 March 2002. As we got down at Jammu airport and walked to the terminal, I recall it occurred to me how infelicitous the grey, gopuram architecture of the terminal looked—though Jammu is a city of temples.

In the maharaja's stately guest house we had the first meeting with chief secretary, Tony Jaitley. As usual preparations for the elections were discussed. Then there was just that suggestion of arrogance in Tony's comment that the time allowed for preparation depended on when the chief minister would like the elections to be held—on which point he was immediately disabused. It was the Election Commission and not the chief minister who decided the election schedule. The chief secretary was a shade crestfallen—the media was then running the story that Farooq Abdullah wanted early elections to contest the elections to the post of Vice-President of India from the platform of re-elected chief minister. Later, I emphasized to the political parties and the media that the Election Commission's visit had nothing to do with early elections, that in fact the elections were far away, that a lot of preliminary work had to be done by us, that free and fair elections were the objective—not any old elections—and that the Election Commission would decide when they would be. It seemed that more than ego was involved when, in the state assembly, the chief minister said the chief election commissioner was wrong and should read the 'rule books' more carefully. Whatever that meant.

The spacious compound had filled with politicians and we met in turn parties like the National Conference, Congress, Bharatiya Janata Party, Peoples Democratic Party, Bahujan Samaj Party and Communist Party of India. From our point of view these were very useful meetings. Most of the comments were on the electoral rolls. They showed us copies of rolls supplied to them for the Jammu bye-elections which had just concluded. These were quite disgraceful— bulky, unwieldy, smudged and illegible. The opposition parties also complained they mostly got copies of the rolls a day or two before polling, while the party in power secured them much earlier. The last intensive revision had been done in 1988 and the electoral rolls consisted of the 1988 mother roll and fourteen supplementary rolls, one for each of the annual summary revisions. So when copies were given to the opposition parties, some of the supplementary rolls were conveniently withheld. The electoral rolls also carried the names of dead voters to facilitate impersonation. The Election Commission's electoral rolls required to be as accurate as the panchayat electoral rolls (panchayat elections had been held earlier). And the electoral rolls ought to be computerized.

The parties also wanted EVMs, identity cards, separate polling stations for migrant Kashmiri Pandits residing in Jammu, Delhi, Udhampur and elsewhere, polling parties from outside the state and adequate security for candidates and party officials. Someone also cautioned the commission against looking for a high percentage of polling as this could be an encouragement to those who might want to rig the elections.

It was easy to promise the electoral rolls would be rectified though at that point in time no one knew how to computerize them. We were also forthcoming on the other requests, barring identity cards. The state had been too turbulent for identity cards to be generated off-line or on-line. In other words, one could not expect voters to congregate at electors' photo identity card centres as in other parts of the country, so another arrangement had to be customized for the state. Some of us, particularly Sayan, had a rough idea which needed fleshing, but it was premature to let it out. From the political parties' perspective these were reassuring meetings. This optimism rubbed off on to the media, and I recall that when a reporter asked what we would do for identity cards, I said we had thought about it and would be shortly finding a solution.

The meeting with the divisional commissioner and deputy commissioners of Jammu Division was disappointing. A meeting is meant to draw out information and perspectives, whereas this one was absurd. When a question was asked, these deputy commissioners would try to anticipate what you wished to hear and answer accordingly. Judging by the alacrity with which they were assuring us everything was fine and safe and normal, they probably thought we needed some cheery reassurance. They could even do intensive revision within a month, when it actually took six to nine months. Scribes could be engaged to copy out the rolls neatly and legibly in two months. The computerization of the rolls would soon follow and the photo identity card programme could begin. (At the same time they advised against pasting draft electoral rolls in polling stations as this would provoke militants to blow up the buildings—they didn't even see they were contradicting themselves.) They didn't know what they were saying, didn't believe we were serious and thought they could get through another loose election with some tall talk. We had had enough, and decided to issue brief directions. Legible copies of the electoral rolls were to be generated through offset printing and these were to be compared with the panchayat rolls in rural areas and death registers in urban areas, to get rid of dead voters.

Srinagar was all subdued light, twirling snowflakes, rusty river and exfoliated plane trees sporting large knobbly seeds and miserable crows. The land had become a slough with persistent cycles of rain, sleet and snow.

We again met the media and political parties and they made the same points as their counterparts in Jammu. But a bearded leader of the PDP delegation, Muzaffar Baig— now finance minister of the state—stood out. He was suave, urbane and flawless in his articulation. At times he was even lyrical. We were not surprised to discover he was a leading counsel in the Supreme Court and an alumnus of the Harvard Law School. We also saw the electoral rolls of Srinagar city—well kept—and some birth and death registers—meticulously maintained in the most elegant Urdu calligraphy.

The commission also had the pleasure of meeting the deputy commissioners of Kashmir Division, three of whom, Abdul Hamid (Srinagar), Basir Khan (Badgam) and Naveen

Choudhury (Baramulla) were to reveal themselves as the most outstanding district officers in the state. It was a brief business-like meeting with the commission giving the same directions as at Jammu.

It had been a satisfying day but exhausting, holed up in one place and draining oneself out on so many people. So Sayan and I went up to Chasm-e-Shahi in the rain and darkness. The fountain was in copious flow and some of us tripped into the channels, while our erratic torch-beams drove the nearby Border Security Force patrols to frenzied challenges. Sayan invested the incident with such frightening hyperbole that Brij (Tandon) thanked the Almighty he hadn't gone with us.

In the morning I was pleasantly surprised to discover in the newspapers that I had already been Kashmiri-ized and that my name was Langdoo. We celebrated it—in wind and falling snow—with a police motorboat ride on an uncharacteristically dour, flagellant Dal Lake and visited one of the bigger house-boat hotels called John Glenn, named after the American astronaut. We were admiring its suites when a fatally bright, temptingly attired—navy blue great coat, suit and tie—Deputy Commissioner Abdul Hamid, who was ushering us, smartly opened a door and thudded down a hatch and out of sight. A plank or two had been removed and he had stepped into the hole and plummeted to the bottom of the boat. Recovered from the shock, we stretched a hand to his speechless, crumpled but miraculously scratchless resurrection.

Soon after, we visited a spare, austere Hazratbal shrine, denuded of people but whirring with pigeons.

The tour ended, the Election Commission got busy with securing what the political parties had demanded. A letter to the chief electoral officer, Jammu and Kashmir of

11 March required: the rolls with supplements to be offset printed; printed copies of the rolls to be distributed to all political parties by 3 April 2002 and prominently displayed; in rural areas, the rolls to be compared with panchayat rolls, and names of dead voters to be eliminated; in municipalities, Notified Area Committees and Town Area Committees the deletion to be on the basis of death registers; where these records did not exist or were not reliable, house-to-house verification to be done; the work to be accomplished by 30 April; an intensive campaign to be launched to net left out voters.

On 18 March in Parliament Prime Minister Vajpayee promised 'fair' elections in Jammu and Kashmir and asked militant groups to participate to 'prove their popularity'. Though encouraging, the reassurance made the commission uneasy. Free and fair elections were exclusively the responsibility of the Election Commission, and the political Executive had refrained from guaranteeing credible elections in every state in India except Jammu and Kashmir. It has been mentioned earlier that Morarji Desai had done so in 1977, and that the fair elections of that year were attributed to him. If the Election Commission did not 'exist' in 1977 the Kashmiri voter would infer from Vajpayee's statement that perhaps it was as much of a non-entity in 2002. However, if the election went wrong, the Election Commission would have to take the entire blame.

Sample copies of the rolls after offset printing were not much of an improvement. On 23 March, Noor Mohammad, chief electoral officer, Uttar Pradesh was again contacted. (In many constituencies in Uttar Pradesh the rolls have to be both in Hindi and in Urdu.) Noor and consultant Kommajosyula Jagannadha Rao—a retired Election

Commission officer who had single-handedly and fearlessly conducted some of the most difficult inquiries in the field and who was ultimately to become the real hero of the elections—visited Jammu, Kathua, Udhampur, Srinagar and Badgam districts. They met the deputy commissioners and were told that the rolls could be handwritten in the Valley but not in Jammu. Computerizing seemed inevitable, but whereas Rao was doubtful that it could be done, Noor Mohammad was confident about it. The job was given to the Uttar Pradesh Urdu Academy, a society under the state government, to do in sixty days. But the trouble was that there was no software for data entry in Urdu in the Nastalik script. Under pressure, Noor remembered there was a 1995 software for data entry in Hindi which he had used. He went to the supplier, retrieved it from a software junkyard as it were, and modified it for use in Urdu. It was a feat in recollection, presence of mind and inventiveness, not normally associated with a bureaucrat in his daily grind.

On 26 March the commission was also talking on telephone to A.N. Ingale, general manager, India Security Press, Nasik, about printing special paper for identity cards. The photo identity cards for Jammu and Kashmir had to have security features of a higher order than the ones produced for the rest of the country. This was necessary to make it difficult for militant organizations to forge them. The commission had decided that the security features should be embodied in the type of paper to be used for the identity card, and the printing on it by the Nasik Press. Since mass photography centres were to be avoided for security reasons, the photographs would have to come from the voter himself, each voter being asked to bring a pair. One photograph would be affixed to the security paper, while the other would be kept in the office records. The details of the voter were to be filled by the taluk revenue official after verification. And then the card was to be issued.

The full commission at its headquarters took a meeting on 8 April with the state's chief electoral officer and deputy commissioners, Srinagar, Badgam and Udhampur. The decisions were: reconstruction of illegible pages of the rolls in Urdu with the help of rolls in Hindi to be completed by 18 April; electoral rolls ready for computerization—those of Badgam, Srinagar and Pulwama districts—to move to Uttar Pradesh by 18 April; names of dead voters to be removed also on the basis of death registers maintained in police stations in rural areas, the process to be completed by 15 May; a committee of deputy election commissioners and chief electoral officers of Uttar Pradesh and Jammu and Kashmir to negotiate rates for computerization; officers from Jammu and Kashmir to go to Uttar Pradesh to test the first checklist of voters after data entry.

Surinder Kumar Mendiratta, by then legal counsel, and Sayan Chatterjee left for Nasik on 15 April. The general manager of the press, Ganga Parkash, went out of his way to be welcoming and accommodating. The requirements would be met on time and the printing would cost a pittance.

On 24 April the commission took a meeting with S.A. Shingle, manager (Designs) of the Nasik Press, the chief electoral officer, Jammu and Kashmir and the deputy commissioner, Badgam, Basir Khan. The design of the card was selected, and it was decided that the entries would be written in black ink by the taluk revenue official. The photo identity card would be laminated with pouches which themselves would carry security features. The pre-printed security paper would indicate the district and the assembly constituency. The number on every identity card would be of eight digits, the first two of which would indicate the constituency number; for example if the voter was shown against Gandarbal assembly constituency, the first two digits after the letters JK would indicate the serial number of Gandarbal assembly constituency, 15. The card would be unilingual, that is, only in English.

A letter of 30 April communicated the decisions to the state's chief electoral officer, chief secretary and the general manager, ISP, Nasik.

The computerization of the state's electoral rolls was not simply entering the electors' names—it meant entry of the electors' details to the extent they were legible, verification of their correctness from the records as well as on the ground, and finally making the required corrections. The checklist obtained from the first data entry was given to the J and K staff that had brought the records to Lucknow and Kanpur (the Kanpur centre was opened later) for comparison with the records and making the necessary corrections. A second checklist was then printed which was sent back to the respective districts in the state for verification in the field. The second checklist, corrected, came back to Uttar Pradesh, was entered into the computer, generating the final printout of the roll (Srinagar, Badgam and Pulwama districts were the first to be done. The remaining eleven districts were not touched until the first three districts had been done correctly.)

The software company was able to prepare the software and operation manual only in the third week of April, and a demonstration-cum-training was organized on 21 April, in which the representatives of twelve agencies participated. Most of the agencies were located in old Lucknow, the

Urdu-speaking rump consisting of Molviganj, Nakkhas, Aminabad, Maqboolganj, Akbarigate and Daliganj. These places are accessible only by two-wheeler or on foot. The twelve agencies had to muster nearly 200 computers and 600 operators to run three shifts, creating a capacity of 200,000 entries per day.

Post-training data entry was done, assembly constituency-wise, further allotment of work to an agency depending on its relative performance.

Close coordination was maintained between the chief electoral officer, Jammu and Kashmir, the chief electoral officer, Uttar Pradesh and the Urdu Academy. And to streamline arrangements further, the Uttar Pradesh government was persuaded to declare the state chief electoral officer in charge of the Urdu Academy as well.

On 6 May the Security Press wanted a formal requisition for the printing work, and the next day the commission intimated them it required pre-formatted security paper for 48,000 cards, the first consignment to be delivered on 6 June. Two days later the commission asked the chief electoral officer, J and K to expedite the placement of the order with the press.

The state government had played passive partner in the matter of identity cards, and the reason became clear when the chief minister visited the commission with adviser Ashok (Tony) Jaitley on one side and director general of police A.K. Suri on the other on 16 May. Farooq began by lightly disclaiming any intention to rig the elections. He said, however, that it was not the right time to launch the EPIC programme. The identity cards might very well be resisted by militant organizations. Alternatively the cards could be forged, creating further complications for the state government. Also women, particularly in the rural areas, would not cooperate. One swiftly reminded him that more than six months earlier he had welcomed having identity cards but had since retreated apparently on the advice of the officers by his side. The DGP tried to intervene and he was ticked off—the Election Commission was not going to allow the Jammu and Kashmir police to run the elections for it. Finally, the chief minister was told that if conditions for issuing the cards were not right, the elections could bide till such conditions obtained. Farooq graciously took the view that if the commission felt so strongly about it, he would go along with it. He wryly wished the programme good luck and facetiously asked us to send him his photograph so that he could get his card made.

The state government continued to hold back despite the chief minister's affirmative. The state home secretary wrote to the commission repeating their objections to the programme. At the same time he suggested that the card could be made more tamper-proof by using a security pouch for lamination.

There was another meeting of the commission with the chief electoral officer and the deputy commissioners of Badgam, Srinagar, Udhampur and Jammu on 30 May. I stressed that all the political parties, including the National Conference, had asked for the cards, and there was no going back on the subject. The decisions were: the commission would prefer that everyone on the electoral roll have a card; applying for a card would be entirely voluntary; the chief electoral officer, district election officers and assistant electoral registration officers would ensure only genuine voters got the card; the elector would fill the prescribed form with two copies of his/her photograph of passport size; how the forms would be collected was left to individual initiative; the cards would be prepared in the offices of the assistant electoral registration officers (tehsildars), and details of electors would be filled by hand in black ink on the blank identity cards supplied by Nasik. The cards would then be laminated; the proper identification of electors would be the responsibility of the electoral registration officers in urban areas and of the assistant electoral registration officers in rural areas; the collection of application forms and issue of identity cards would be from 15 June to 15 July.

To put a final seal on the matter, K.J. Rao and the chief electoral officer visited Nasik and finalized the schedule of despatches of the blank identity cards—the first lot by 6 June, the second lot by 7 June and the third by 25 June. The cost of the first despatch, Rs. 50,000, was paid by the commission to expedite things.

All the 9,000 EVMs required were received and stocked in the period—April to May.

On 3 June another letter went to the chief secretary indicating the commission was not impressed by the state governments' objections to the identity card and was willing to take the risk of some hostility from the militants. But more importantly, the Election Commission's directions to the state government on matters of electoral management were addressed to the permanent Executive—headed by the chief secretary—for implementation, and there was no scope for the directives to be deliberated with the political Executive. The stocks of pre-printed formats of identity cards in Nasik were to be lifted without demur, and the cost borne by the state. Fortunately I.S. Malhi, an ex-serviceman, who was going to demit office in October 2002, and had decided that he would do a first-rate election and retire with honour, had taken over on 30 April as chief secretary and within a month of his settling down this curt letter had its effect.

By 12 June the commission had already approved the chief electoral officer's recommendation for superior micron film for lamination pouches.

On 13 June the commission put out a press note on action taken till then. Apart from summarizing what had been done with the electoral rolls, EVMs, identity cards, rationalization of polling stations (not more than three polling stations in one building, and no voter to have to walk more than two kilometres to the polling station), and providing equitable security to the political parties to enable them to campaign freely, the commission also promised to issue voter slips, hitherto left to the political parties everywhere in India (voter slips told the electors which polling stations they had to go to). It was also mentioned that since the commission's visit in March, somebody or the other had been to the state on a monthly basis. Taruvai Subbayya Krishna Murthy, election commissioner, who had not been in March, had gone there in May.

The very next day there was a meeting in the commission in which the establishment officer, Department of Personnel, Government of India, agreed to spare officers to function as special observers. (The special observer was a new functionary thought up, so to say, specially for the state, and he was not merely to observe the elections but to go well in advance to the allotted constituency, ensure implementation of the commission's instructions on the electoral rolls, EVMs, identity cards, security of party functionaries . . . as well as a level playing field in terms of getting rid of those that were partisan among the crucial functionaries in the operation). In nine years the commission had travelled from where it had had to go to the Supreme Court to get ordinary observers to the point where it could have its own nominees as special observers.

The identity card distribution programme began on 15 June.

On 16 June the Election Commission visited the state again (Lyngdoh, Tandon and Sayan Chatterjee, this time reinforced by Ajay Jha). In Srinagar we stayed at Raj Bhavan, a modest wooden building which creaked continuously with the wind that filled its rafters and a generous, terraced garden then waxing with the full range of seasonal flowers against a green backdrop paled with rain. And the cuckoo was in song.

The first meeting was with the deputy commissioners of Srinagar Division at which the different items of work were reviewed.

In the computerization of electoral rolls the progress was found satisfactory except for one or two districts where even the first-round verification had not been done.

On identity cards the assessment was that there would be a good response. However, a doubt was expressed that asking electors to bring their photographs might lead to a lower turnout where photographers were not available.

The deputy commissioners were all ready to receive the electronic voting machines at their district headquarters. (The dispersal of EVMs from Jammu was not to be taken lightly, and it was one of our fears that the militants could blow up some of the trucks in which they were conveyed. The work had to be done quietly under proper security.) In the matter of training in the use of the EVM, the deputy commissioners were asked to follow the given schedule and include the political parties and media. They were also to involve engineers in the PWD and other departments who could form part of the core group of trainers in the state. But what made that meeting unique was that I rather loudly and rudely articulated two things the very mention of which was forbidden in the Valley . . . and so shook the deputy commissioners out of their skin; the Election Commission was totally indifferent to the percentage of voting and would not tolerate anyone being forced to vote by people in uniform or otherwise; the interests of India and Kashmir were not inevitably linked to the Abdullahs and the elections were open to other possibilities. The Election Commission was determined that the voter would actually decide this.

Finally, I did demand that the 2002 elections be at least as fair as the 1977 elections.

Then we met the political parties. The Communist Party (Marxist) wanted: election under governor's rule; polling parties from outside the state; every candidate provided with security; a polling station in every village (people were reluctant to go to another village to vote); Central paramilitary forces for manning polling stations; proper observers;

The National Conference wanted: maximum participation and therefore proper security for the voters; de-clubbing polling stations which had been concentrated in the 1996 elections for security reasons (with the consequent dispersal people would not have to walk more than two kilometres to the polling stations).

The Congress delegation was led by a very witty but agreeable lawyer. The Congress wanted: the 'National Defence Force' and 'State Task Force' to be disbanded (the 'NDF' consisted of 2,000 militant renegades maintained only to harass them, the opposition parties claimed—in Anantnag they had put up bills in conspicuous places threatening opposition leaders with death; the 'STF' consisted of a majority of renegades and a minority of notorious police officers, some of whom began life as crooks); identity cards to be given to everybody (these were being confined to National Conference voters); security at par with the National Conference (personal security officer, vehicle and accommodation); polling parties from outside the state and returning officers from the state Indian Administrative Service cadre; separate polling stations for Pandit migrants; polling stations to be manned by the Border Security Force/Central Reserve Police Force.

The BJP demanded: the identity card be made multi-purpose, and the period for its distribution be extended; elections be held only under governor's rule; security for candidates and party workers be at par with that extended to their National Conference counterparts; deputy commissioners and senior superintendents of police be replaced wholesale before the polls.

The Awami League wanted: the 'NDF' to be disbanded (the 'NDF' were ex-militants each paid Rs. 4,000 per month from Security Related Expenditure); identity cards to be made multi-purpose; training in the use of the EVM.

The Peoples Democratic Party demanded: the revision of the electoral rolls be done properly (the political parties had not been provided with the electoral rolls. Form 6 was not being accepted anywhere; also, in Srinagar, door-to-door verification had not been done.); identity cards to be made multi-purpose; polling stations be de-clubbed.

The Bahujan Samaj Party wanted: a multi-purpose identity card; security at par with the National Conference; de-clubbing of polling stations; inter-district reshuffling of officers concerned with the elections.

In the meeting with the chief secretary, director general of police and home secretary the following emerged: the state police strength was only 300 companies; the requirement of Central paramilitary forces was 450 companies; Jammu and Kashmir police would handle anti-militant operations; the CPMF would be deployed for election-related security; the army would provide area domination.

That evening there was a dinner for the Election Commission at Government House at which the military, civil and police heads were present. It was a curious event as, no matter which corner of the room or whom you spoke to—barring an exception or two—you could not work yourself out of the tedious refrain: Kashmiris were patriotic Indians like everyone else; the position was improving with some 1,000 militants out of 3,000 accounted for; India's interest lay in the continuance of Farooq as chief minister. I later checked with my colleagues and found they had had the same experience. Was the dinner calculated to make us doubt what I had told the deputy commissioners during the day, or to neutralize us for the press conference the following day, or to serve both purposes? One was amazed at the crudeness and stupidity of the impresario behind it all (someone from the Intelligence Bureau?), but even more so that so many political parties had asked for elections under governor's rule.

One has already mentioned an inquiry about whether the commission proposed to have foreign observers and the decision in the negative. A sensitivity to the subject in the commission had, however, survived and at one time it even proposed to consult an acknowledged Kashmir expert like journalist Prem Shankar Jha.

There was therefore an all-embracing openness in the way I began the press conference on the 17th morning: anybody from anywhere in the world could come and see the elections, but there would be only hand-picked Indian civil servants as official observers; there would be complete access to the polling stations for the media, national and international, as well as the diplomatic corps; the commission had given directions to the Ministry of Home Affairs on the security to be provided to the workers/candidates of political parties; uniformed forces were not to compel anybody to vote—compulsion an offence to be visited by prosecution. They were there to reassure voters and create conducive conditions; 8,000 EVMs had been procured and their use would prevent a lot of booth-capturing and rigging; identity cards specially designed for Jammu and Kashmir—two photographs from each voter, one for the record and the other pasted on security paper from Nasik and laminated— would be used. The details in the application form would be verified by the tehsildars before the identity cards were delivered; the electoral rolls initially illegible and carrying the names of dead voters had been rectified. Thanks to the chief electoral officer of Uttar Pradesh who had found the software, even the computerization of the rolls was about to be completed; a by-product of this was the generation of voter slips. For the first time in Indian electoral history, the commission would be distributing voter slips—details on pieces of paper showing the polling stations specific electors had to go to vote—instead of the political parties; opposition parties had accused the government of using the 'STF' and 'NDF' to harass them and disrupt their political activity; requests had also been made for the wholesale transfer of deputy commissioners and superintendents of police before the elections.

Despite no licence being allowed—for security reasons— by the Department of Telecom to anyone to set up mobile phone services in Jammu and Kashmir the speed with which the Srinagar press conference got to the principal metropolises of the world was breath-taking. On the way to the airport one was already being pursued by somebody from the BBC in London wanting to talk on satellite phone.

In the meeting with the deputy commissioners of Jammu Division the points regarding the dissociation of India's and Kashmir's interests from the Abdullahs' and the avoidance of compulsion on voters to vote were repeated. In the review of the preparations for the elections it was emphasized that Jammu Division was far behind in data entry work in Uttar Pradesh, and therefore had to improve.

The deputy commissioners wanted a de-clubbing of polling stations and indicated a corresponding increase in the requirement of security forces.

In the meeting with political parties the BJP wanted: free identity cards, the voter being reimbursed for the two photographs taken from him; duplicate entries in the electoral rolls to be eliminated; polling personnel from outside the state; Central paramilitary forces to be used for election duty; separate polling stations for migrant voters since postal ballots were being manipulated.

The Bahujan Samaj Party demanded: reimbursement of the cost of the photographs for the identity cards; security at par with National Conference office-bearers; elections under governor's rule; Central paramilitary forces/Punjab police for electoral duty; strict checking of election expenses; the transfer of special police officer Akhnoor, Jagjeet Singh Jagga.

The Congress wanted: observers in every assembly constituency; minimum security to political parties to be ensured; polling parties from outside the state; Central paramilitary forces in all polling stations; free identity cards; separate polling stations for migrant voters; polling stations within two kilometres; election under governor's rule; special police officers to be left out of election duty;

observers not to accept the state government's hospitality.

The CPI(M) demanded a free identity card and mixed polling personnel from inside and outside the state.

The Janta Dal United asked for the reconciliation of the voters' lists in Urdu with those in Hindi.

The National Conference asked for a de-clubbing of the polling stations and a free identity card.

The Panthers Party wanted the electoral rolls to be corrected and elections under governor's rule.

The Rashtriya Janta Dal desired: elections under governor's rule; corrections in the electoral rolls; and security for candidates.

The *Kashmir Times*' reaction to the Srinagar press conference was: 'The Chief Election Commissioner's ludicrous claim that the forthcoming election to the State assembly will be more fair than even the 1977 poll can only be accepted with a pinch of salt . . .' No one claimed anything, least of all because it was impossible to 'claim' that an event in the future would be one way or the other. They probably meant 'promise', but the word was not used in the press conference. I had told the deputy commissioners in our meeting with them that the 2002 elections had to be at least as fair as the 1977 elections. This was evidently leaked to the print media, who gave it a dramatic twist to make sure that no one missed the point that the biggest buffoon was in town.

The *Hindu* was determined to selectively insert foreign observers into 'anybody from anywhere in the world could come to see the elections . . .'

The *Indian Express* saw the Election Commission as a tool in 'a carefully thought-out strategy by New Delhi which seeks to inspire confidence in the Jammu and Kashmir electorate and ensure a decent voter turnout in a free and fair election' (as if you needed a conspiracy for such an unexceptionable objective). The Election Commission was also offering a sop to diplomats and the international media, but only as individuals, not as 'election observers for any foreign organization or country'.

Whether one was a tool of the Government of India or not, there was little that could be remedied by contradiction. It was both necessary and possible, however, to make a clarification on 'foreign observers'. The opportunity was the Jammu press conference of 18 June. Under the Indian law only senior civil servants could be election observers. And their function was not merely to observe but to intervene and correct the course of events where needed. However, the commission would allow access to the polling stations to the media, diplomatic corps and representatives of Election Commissions of countries with sound democratic credentials in their individual capacities.

{22}

Mid-June to Mid-August 2002—
Fulfilling Demands and More

On 19 June the security pouch for the lamination of the identity cards was approved.

By 22 June Sayan Chatterjee, Ajay Jha and I were once again in the state, but this time in Leh.

At the meeting with the chief electoral officer and deputy commissioners of Leh and Kargil it transpired that: the 400 EVMs required for Leh and 300 for Kargil were already available; so too were 100 EVMs needed for training; training would begin on 24 June; computerized rolls would be available by the end of the month; there was a serious shortage of photographers for the two photographs required for each voter's identity card.

There was a common meeting with all political parties, that is, the National Conference, Congress and BJP. They wanted: the cost of the photographs on the identity cards to be reimbursed; government photographers to be employed in the interior as no others would be found; a polling station in Leh with 1,500 voters to complete its voting within the outer limit of 4.00 p.m. (the confusion among the voters about which polling stations they had to go to usually necessitated polling till 7.00 p.m. It was hoped that the voter slips to be issued by the commission would rectify this); indelible ink in stock to be checked as in certain places in the 1999 Lok Sabha elections the indelible ink was not effective; observers to tour the interior and spend more time in the constituency; subdivisional magistrates to be authorized, in addition to tehsildars, to issue identity cards.

Later one crossed the highest motorable pass in the subcontinent—the 18,380 ft. Khardong-la—and bowled down to the Nobra Valley, adopted home of the double-humped Bactrian camel, and then to Diskit, one of the subdivisional headquarters. Diskit had only two photographers to take snaps for identity cards. An extract of my tour note read:

> Diskit is an arbored settlement of 1,800 people— including 100 monks of the local monastery (Many villages in Bihar are thrice as numerous). There are only 1039 voters. Their Polling Station (No.18) is in the local high school which is provided with water supply, electricity and a dry latrine. There were complaints of inaccuracies in the parental entries in the electoral roll, of dead people in the electoral roll and of misleading posters showing religious leaders in the company of individual candidates. And there are only two photographers to take the identity card pictures for the entire electorate in the subdivision.
>
> Up the Indus is the other subdivisional headquarters, Nyoma—no photographer in that part of the world.

On 26 June the Election Commission asked the Ministry of Home Affairs for information on the 'NDF', 'STF', 'SPO' and 'SOG' of Jammu and Kashmir. Some twenty days later the state government, through the Ministry of Home Affairs, denied the existence of the 'National Defence Force'.

By 1 July the rolls of all the assembly constituencies had been computerized. But before then there had been a lot of excitement. The officers from Srinagar had been the first to arrive in Lucknow, with raw electoral rolls, in the third week of April. They found the heat unbearable, especially when they were dossed in a downtown hotel at discounted rates. Nothing appetizing came with such Noor Mohammad-inspired economy. Tempers ran so high that the data-entry vendors had to provide lodgings in their office premises and open temporary kitchens.

The officers from Jammu outdid them. They arrived at the hottest time of the year—in May. (A self-appointed leader was miffed at everything he saw, but admitted it was the heat that had got him down.) They wouldn't stir, they said, unless they could stay and work in cooler surroundings. A data-entry vendor with unusual presence of mind downloaded the day's temperature in Jammu from the internet—it was almost identical with Lucknow's—and cheerfully passed it on to the busybody and that fairly quelled the rebellion.

The computerization of the rolls in Lucknow and Kanpur was deliberately done as quietly as possible so as not to attract any reprisal from militant groups. But there had been no briefing, and the secretary of the Urdu Academy saw no reason why his institution should have done work of such earth-shaking importance without telling the world about it. His statement appeared on a TV channel, and the Uttar Pradesh electoral establishment shrivelled. It was then busily whispered that this activity was not to be talked about.

The embassies were not slow to respond to the June press conferences in Srinagar and Jammu. The first was the

New Zealand High Commission. The high commissioner, Caroline McDonald, called on the commission on 2 July to confirm that diplomats would be given free access to the polling stations in Jammu and Kashmir.

*

On 4 and 5 July I was at a seminar on 'Electoral Democracy' in Cambridge. The seminar included academics and heads of election commissions from some of the Commonwealth countries.

Everyone was impressed not only with the virility of Indian democracy, but with the effectiveness of the Election Commission of India in handling an electorate of 640 million people. More particularly with the Model Code of Conduct—which had no formal legal sanction but which was implicitly recognized by the court and obeyed by all political parties—which not only brought discipline into the elections but whittled away the advantages of the government, especially the unfair ones like appointing people and sanctioning projects just before the elections.

What was considered unique was that the Election Commission fixed all election schedules on its own without even feigning the courtesy of consulting the Government of India or state governments.

Also, nothing was better proof of the freedom of action of the commission than its order of 28 June—in deference to the Supreme Court's order, no doubt, but in disregard of the government request for time to consult all political parties—requiring each candidate to disclose by affidavit: whether he had been convicted/acquitted/discharged of any criminal offence in the past, and if convicted, whether he had been punished with imprisonment or fine; prior to six months of the filing of the nomination, whether the candidate had been accused of an offence with imprisonment of two years or more, and whether charges had been framed or cognizance taken by the court; if so, the details thereof; his assets (immovable, movable, bank balances, etc.) and those of his spouse and dependants; his liabilities in relation to government and financial institutions; his educational qualifications. It was well known that the assembly elections in Jammu and Kashmir were near and it was reassuring to the group to have an Election Commission as independent as the one in India to conduct them.

Returned to London on 6 July I got an SOS from the high commissioner, Ronen Sen. Would I attend a dinner in one of the Indian restaurants to convince Lord Dholakia of the Liberal Democrats, Andrew Whitehead of BBC—who had had a stint in India—and Simon Long of the *Economist* that there was a distinction between the Election Commission of India and the Government of India even when it came to Kashmir? Fresh from the Cambridge seminar and animated by a couple of whiskies, it seems I did not do too badly.

*

On 11 July the Election Commission decided to accept the chief secretary, Jammu and Kashmir's proposal to reimburse the voter for the cost of his photographs for the identity card. The reimbursement was kept at Rs. 15 and it was hoped that it would enhance the already warm response to the cards.

British high commissioner Rob Young visited the commission on 11 July. Apart from confirming that diplomats were welcome to see the elections in J and K he had more than a passing interest in elections in Gujarat. There was more than a week to go for the dissolution of the Gujarat assembly, but speculations on it were rife.

July 11 was also the day of briefing for the special observers. There were twenty of them—four from the Bihar cadre—and they were a very select group even among observers. They were to be distributed two each for Baramulla, Srinagar and Jammu and one per every other district.

They were alerted to the unusual political circumstances of the state, the importance of a free and fair election and the demand for 'international observers' which was turned down for the reason that the Indian electoral law did not provide for them. Observers were already provided under the law, and many of them had functioned as observers before. Observers in India were superior to 'international observers' in that it was their duty to make crucial interventions to correct the course of events in the electoral process. (The 'international observer', on the other hand, just noted.) The special observer, however, was specially conceived for the almost impossibly difficult conditions of Jammu and Kashmir. He or she would not only be an extension of the Election Commission, but of the state administration at a very senior level to get the tailor-made measures—like the production and distribution of Nasik Press security paper-based identity cards and the distribution of voter slips—implemented before polling. In the Jammu and Kashmir context it was also vital to have the newly computerized electoral rolls distributed to the political parties in time, as well as to get the training in the unfamiliar EVM completed in every corner of the state, no matter how riddled with militancy.

The special observer would have to supervise all this

and also help the commission to get rid of all elements within the field administration that were disruptive of fair elections. All special observers were required to make at least three visits to the state before the elections were notified. Thereafter, they would function like ordinary observers. The special observers first descended on the state two days after the briefing.

The commission issued another press note on 12 July. The polling stations clubbed together in 1996 for security reasons were being dispersed to the locations indicated in the electoral rolls of 1988. This would mean 900 additional polling stations, but voters would not have to walk more than two kilometres.

In the Lok Sabha elections of 1998 and '99, Kashmiri Pandit migrants from the Valley were a notified class of voters, allowed to use the postal ballot. Since there were complaints of considerable delay in the transmission of postal ballot papers to the returning officers resulting in a significant percentage of the notified class of voters being deprived of their voting rights, arrangements were being made for the migrants to vote through electronic voting machines in polling stations set up at their camps in Jammu and Delhi.

Electoral rolls of all eighty-seven assembly constituencies had been computerized in Urdu, and copies were being distributed free to all recognized political parties in the state. In deference to requests from registered unrecognized parties, those which had a legislative presence in the state would, as a special case, each be supplied a free copy of the electoral rolls. The Peoples Democratic Party, Jammu and Kashmir Awami League and Jammu and Kashmir National Panthers Party would be the beneficiaries.

During the commission's visit to the state the most

common grievance was that whereas leaders of the ruling party were holding ministerial and other important offices and were entitled to heavy security and could campaign freely, leaders of opposition parties did not have this privilege. The commission had got the Union government to direct the state government to provide security cover, at state cost, to one leader of each recognized national and state party—that is, recognized in the state—in each of the districts in the Valley, as well as in the districts of Doda, Rajouri, Poonch and Jammu. This would benefit the BSP, BJP, CPI, CPI(M), Congress and National Congress.

Twenty special observers were being deputed from the following week.

On 16 July it was the turn of the ambassador of Japan, Hiroshi Hirabayashi, to meet the commission about Jammu and Kashmir and Gujarat. He volunteered ex-US-President, Jimmy Carter as a potential international observer in Jammu and Kashmir, but I promptly shot down the proposal saying that according to the Web, Jimmy Carter was fond of going to countries which had a habit of rigging elections and with the kind of presidential elections the United States had last had, he would be better occupied at home.

*

The Jammu and Kashmir and Gujarat assembly elections were originally due to be five months adrift of each other, and normally should not have been associated. However, the Gujarat assembly was to be prematurely dissolved, and the elections in the two states brought closer to each other. Not that this had to happen to make the BJP liken the situations in Gujarat and Jammu and Kashmir. To that party there was no difference between disturbances caused by communal riots in Gujarat and those by militancy in Jammu and Kashmir. If elections in Jammu and Kashmir were being held as scheduled, why should the Election Commission hesitate in having early elections in Gujarat in pursuance of a premature dissolution of the assembly? This, to us, was like saying what was so special about Muslims being killed or driven out of Gujarat when Kashmiri Pandits had been systematically killed or driven out of the Kashmir Valley—that they had to be treated differently?

The nearness of the two elections was to make the international community see them together as challenges to the secularism of Indian society as well as the probity of the Indian polity. The Indian educated middle class was generally to think the same way.

There were to be other equally important unforeseen connections as a result of changing relationships between the Election Commission and the Government of India on one hand, and between the commission and the media, particularly the electronic media, on the other.

The connections will reveal themselves as we go along.

For quite some time before it happened there were strong rumours that the government of Gujarat would have the governor prematurely dissolve the assembly to compel the commission to hold elections before the first week of October—perhaps to coincide with the Jammu and Kashmir elections—under Article 174(1) of the Constitution. (This article requires that between the last sitting in one session of a state legislature and the first sitting in the next session less than six months should have elapsed.) The Gujarat assembly had last met on 4 April 2002. The commission, which had been kept abreast of the communal riots and their effects by the chief electoral officer of Gujarat, was concerned about the large-scale migration of voters from their ordinary places of residence—where they had been registered as voters—and was therefore not inclined to hold elections in a hurry. It saw its duty was to bring about a situation by which the displaced voters would not only be accounted for, but provided voting facilities where they had shifted.

At 11.00 a.m. on 19 July, I.K. Gujral, a former prime minister, B.G. Verghese, Swami Agnivesh, Justice Rajinder Sachar, Syeda Hamid and Harsh Mander met the commission and raised the following issues on Gujarat: electoral rolls were not reliable; officials involved in the riots had yet to be transferred; relief camps were being forcibly closed to make it appear that things had become normal; the Gujarati language media was up to mischief; the commission ought not to hold early elections even if the House were prematurely dissolved.

I told the group there would not be any early elections. After which Gujral seems to have immediately conveyed what I said to the media.

At 12.30 p.m., Arun Jaitley, then ex-law minister, sought an appointment for himself and was given 3.00 p.m. The commission had also learnt that the Gujarat government was to have a Cabinet meeting at 4.00 p.m. to consider the dissolution of the assembly. Jaitley was alone and pleasantries extended to discussing the elections in Jammu and Kashmir. Then Jaitley urged early elections in Gujarat because, according to him, normalcy had returned to the state. In support of his point he cited the closing down of relief camps and the holding of local bodies' elections. My reply— the camps had been shut down not because they were no longer required but to suggest normalcy. The affected persons were still in the vicinity of the closed camps, had not gone home and were being looked after by non-government organizations.

Jaitley then mentioned K.P.S. Gill as supporting the cause for early elections. My response—I too had been in service, knew about Gill, and there was no need to discuss him. Inwardly I was noting all that cynicism with distaste.

Jaitley thereafter drew a parallel between Gujarat and Jammu and Kashmir, and said there was no reason why there should not be early elections in Gujarat if there was an early dissolution of the House. In fact Article 324 was circumscribed by Article 174, and the commission would have to hold elections well before the first week of October. He cited the examples of Punjab and Assam as states where elections were held even before normalcy had returned. There had to be an end to this sophistry, and I said that the difference was that in the case of Gujarat we were dealing with a discredited government. He accused me of using political language. I replied that language of that kind was not a politician's prerogative. 'We have lost all faith in the commission,' he said, and stomped out of the room.

Jaitley evidently did not speak to the media about the outcome of this meeting before the Gujarat assembly was dissolved. From our point of view we wondered why he had come alone, or whom he was representing. We assumed, however, that he had told Gujarat chief minister Narendra Modi about it. In any event the Gujarat assembly was dissolved at 5.30 p.m. the same day.

The Congress delegation under Manmohan Singh saw the commission on 22 July. It made the following points: the Gujarat assembly should not have been prematurely dissolved; camps were being forcibly closed despite many people needing shelter; no relief and rehabilitation work was going on; there was great fear and anxiety among Muslims; the riots were still on, the last outbreak having occurred a few days earlier in Viramgam; Article 174(1) did not apply after an assembly had been dissolved, and the Election Commission, under Article 324, not only had the freedom, but the obligation to wait till there was a conducive environment for free and fair elections.

In the 23 July issue of the *Economic Times* there was a tendentious caption, 'Tandon, Krishnamurthy disagree with Lyngdoh'. The associated report mentioned my being against an early Gujarat poll, and quoted me in an interview with *Outlook* magazine—'The people who talk of early elections have no authority . . . so, if a few mad people keep talking about it, why should we bother.' According to the report, I did not budge despite Arun Jaitley's having met the commission and explained how Article 324 was circumscribed by Article 174 and the home secretary's having been twice to the commission to assure it that adequate security forces could be arranged. (There appeared to be a division between my colleagues and me.) The BJP would, however, continue the pressure on the commission— patently this report was part of it—and its president, Venkaiah Naidu, would visit the commission the following day. There was also a story to the effect that the Union Cabinet had decided to add two more members to the Election Commission.

The following morning Naidu called with Jaitley in tow. When we said we were sending a team to ascertain facts in Gujarat, Jaitley accused me of having already decided against early elections. But Naidu cut him short and said he hoped I would not be sticking to the point I made in the interview with *Outlook*. My reply was that that was before the dissolution of the Gujarat assembly. Now that it had been dissolved and we were sending a team, we had an open mind on the matter.

The Left parties and Janata Dal(S) called on 25 July.

Besides repeating the points raised by the Congress, they said names had been deleted from the electoral roll. Also, there had been large-scale destruction of dwellings and people had migrated.

The same day Sahmat, an NGO, dropped in and said the state government was a party to the carnage and that a large number of people did not want to go back to their villages. First Information Reports had not been registered with the police. Article 174 was not binding as elections could be held only when conditions normalized.

M.L. Sondhi, an ex-diplomat-turned-politician, came in on the 26th and wanted the Election Commission to assess conditions on the ground before deciding. He even thought the commission should assume the function of governing, as the caretaker government had no legal basis. The Jan Shakti party also met the commission and wanted elections to be held later.

*

A dinner meeting in Ashok Hotel on 26 July with the home secretary, expenditure secretary and defence secretary, Government of India, and the chief secretary, finance secretary and chief electoral officer of Jammu and Kashmir worked out the modalities for bringing polling staff from Uttar Pradesh and Punjab to Jammu and Kashmir, and funds required for the purpose.

The chief secretary and finance secretary, Jammu and Kashmir, suggested that one officer from outside the state per polling party, instead of the two mentioned in the note for discussion, would be sufficient. Since the state was unfamiliar with EVMs, and so many political parties had asked for polling parties from other states, it was decided that there would be two officers per polling party from outside Jammu and Kashmir.

The crux of the matter was, of course, the funding of the operation. The Union home secretary was quite sure the project could not be funded from the Security Related Expenditure Account. The finance secretary, Jammu and Kashmir, countered that in 1996 such expenditure was indeed met from this account. The state government for its part was ready to provide personnel for all the polling parties. But since the Election Commission had insisted on half the personnel from outside the state, funds for the outsiders should come from the Government of India. In the event, who should foot the bill was deferred, but it was decided that the Government of India would be giving a 'special ways and means' advance to get the operation underway. And since the polling personnel would be coming from Uttar Pradesh and Punjab, the ways and means advance would be apportioned between the two states.

The Uttar Pradesh parties would be flying to the Valley, and it was decided it would be easier to get them there by air force rather than chartered planes. Whether the costs would be waived or paid directly by the Government of India to the air force, was left to the appropriate departments to decide.

Since the Punjabis were no longer of the generation that knew Urdu, they could only go to Jammu—by road. Having got to Jammu by bus they would be under the security cover of the Jammu and Kashmir government, as indeed the Uttar Pradesh party would be once they got to the Valley. The polling parties from both states would board and lodge in security camps, and move only with armed protection.

Linking the incentives to the polling personnel with their salary was discouraged by the Jammu and Kashmir government as this had created complications in the past. So lump sum ex-gratia payment was proposed. This would be Rs. 10,000 for three phases and Rs. 7,000 for two phases. For other quanta of duty, for example, one phase, being in reserve, etc. the commission would decide how much should be paid.

Other incentives would be at the 1996 level: Rs. 5,00,000 in case of death on duty plus an appropriate job to a dependant of the deceased/nominee at a place of his or her choice; Rs. 25,000 for permanent disability and Rs. 10,000 for temporary disability; DA @ one and a half times the rate applicable to Central government employees or Rs. 135 per day; free board and lodging with the respective CPMF; medical aid/hospitalization at the cost of the state government; advance drawals upto 80 per cent of entitlement.

The requirement of polling personnel from each state was pegged at 2,500, and the advances to Uttar Pradesh and Punjab were calculated at Rs. 34,000,000 to each.

Separately with the Jammu and Kashmir officers it was decided that Kashmiri migrants who were not able to go to the polling stations set up in the camps at Jammu, Delhi, etc. would be given the option to vote by postal ballot.

By 31 July all voter slips for the state had been printed. The electoral rolls had been consolidated—the 1988 mother roll and fourteen supplementaries. But in the short time available, integrating rolls or grouping voters household-wise was not possible. This function was performed by the voter slips. Depending on the number of voters in each household, there were three categories of slips—with ten or less voters printed on a quarter page, with eleven to twenty voters on a half page, and with twenty-one to forty voters on a full page. The voter slip also indicated the relevant polling station and assembly constituency. One part of it was for the voter to mention if any member of the household had been left out. Similarly, the details of voters who had died were to be given. Since the identity card programme had just started it was intended that voter slips would also serve for identification at the polling station.

In all 351,850 pages were printed—each page having been checked by the Urdu Academy staff—a trail being maintained to fix responsibility for any negligence. Four thousand pages had to be reprinted because of subsequent careless handling.

The first lot was transported by road, but the later ones by air, recognition of the importance of the slips being responsible for the transition.

*

There had been horrific communal riots in Gujarat after the burning of a railway compartment in Godhra—on 27 February 2002—and charring of fifty-seven 'kar sevaks' inside it returning from Ayodhya. A wanton killing of Muslims and destruction and looting of their property ensued. What distinguished these riots from the earlier ones in Gujarat was not only the almost complete absence of state intervention, but extensive police connivance with the rioters, particularly in north and central Gujarat.

The electronic and print media covered the riots as no events in India had ever been covered before, news channels deputing their teams to all parts of the state. The coverage persevered for months without a break, and contrary to the state government's claim of having controlled the riots, reported fresh incidents as well as brought to light the gruesome, inhuman and barbaric conditions in the relief camps where the riot victims had been sheltered. The transparent and positive coverage of the events iterated the splendid work done by the same media a year earlier when an earthquake had ravaged large parts of Kutch, Saurashtra and central Gujarat. Among the most noteworthy were Star News (NDTV) journalists Rajdeep Sardesai and Barkha Dutt.

When the commission's nine-member team led by deputy election commissioners Shailendra Mendiratta and Ajay Jha went on a fact-finding inquiry to Gujarat (30 July to 4 August) the primary concern was how to get an accurate picture of the electoral ground situation, in a context where the state government had chosen to deny or refute all allegations of its connivance in fanning the riots and taking an active role through the police. Relief camps were being closed and inmates forced to return to their homes, which were in shambles. And even the National Human Rights Commission had been given short shrift when probing human rights violations connected with the riots. If the commission had left the itinerary to the state government, its team would have done a conducted tour of 'sterilized' areas.

If the team had chalked out its own programme and passed it on to the state government there was every likelihood that local officials would be dispersed in advance to tutor people in the language and propaganda of the government.

In short the Election Commission, like every other institution that had dealt with some aspect or the other of the riots, was confronted with a hostile state government, quite satisfied with its handiwork, and therefore determined to prevaricate or mislead or lie or even barricade but not to cooperate.

On the other hand, the victims had been shattered, and were not likely to be forthcoming with any information. The question was how to gain their confidence and draw them out of themselves.

The team chose to disclose the day's programme in the morning. The choice of places to visit was made on the basis of media, NHRC and NGO reports. The places were divided district-wise, each team of three members being assigned a group of districts.

But it wasn't the state government alone that had to be negotiated. The media had gathered in very large numbers the moment the team landed in Ahmedabad. The team tried to stay aloof but its pursuers were not to be shaken off either at the airport or Circuit House despite the state's having been plunged in darkness by a failure of the western power grid.

Since it was inevitable, it was decided that the team should meet and tell them it was there to assess to what extent conditions existed for free and fair elections. To find out where the Election Commission officers would be going they were told to assemble in the morning, so that the programme could be given to them. Nevertheless, the media could scarcely contain its impatience, and but for the blackout, the team might not have slept at all on the 30th night.

On the morning of the 31st both electronic and print media choked the Circuit House. Almost every news channel and newspaper was represented. Given the programme, they were told they had a choice of following any of the three teams. It was made clear to them that no opinions or views of any of the commission representatives could be sought. Ajay would be the commission's spokesman, and they were free to report and film the day's proceedings in detail.

For the media this was a boon, as the local administration had restricted their visits to the relief camps. (The curbs made sense when the team met the chief secretary, when he recited his catechism of complete normalcy and railed against the distorted projections of the media—particularly the English language print and electronic media.) The Election Commission was in town and all media restraints had disappeared. Wherever the three teams went they started a spate of media persons in cars, on scooters and motorcycles and shook the countryside alive.

The media in such great number had the remarkable effect of a wall behind which savaged human beings could shed their fear and relate their sorrows. In the first location, which was a camp marked for closure by the administration, the camp organizer and a revenue official were initially the only ones who met the team. But soon after, in the friction and heat generated by the camera teams and scribes, the camp inmates poured from every direction relating their stories. The dumbed-down camp organizer suddenly transformed, found his tongue, and elaborated on their sufferings. Even when the teams ventured into affected, but unrecorded localities, the media continued to play pied piper and to lend seriousness to the inquiry. Delegations materialized and spoke against the government, particularly the police, relief measures, the manner in which the camps were running . . .

A symbiosis had suddenly developed between the media and the team.

The teams also met BJP delegations which made the familiar point—if elections in Kashmir why not in Gujarat?

The teams covered twelve of the twenty-five districts in the state and touched most of the affected areas. They observed that the electoral rolls in the state, revised with reference to 1 January 2002 were, in many cases, no longer valid, as a large number of voters had shifted from houses and localities where they were ordinarily resident and had not returned. This was because their houses had been totally demolished, burnt or otherwise damaged, or the law and order situation had not mended, or both. They also found there was still a sense of insecurity among the displaced persons, and it was not reasonable to expect them to shed their fear psychosis and venture to the polling stations to cast their votes.

The team concluded that an election on such defective electoral rolls and in such a traumatic setting would not only deprive many voters of their franchise, but encourage unscrupulous people to impersonate them. The elections would have to wait as they would need to be preceded by confidence-building measures.

*

After nearly five months of preparation, the Jammu and Kashmir elections were announced on 2 August. The litany of things done by the commission was again recited in the press note, namely, clean and computerized electoral rolls, EVMs in place, polling stations being rationalized, equity in security to political parties, customized identity cards for Jammu and Kashmir, voter slips, separate polling stations for migrant Pandits and special observers. In the revision of the electoral rolls 200,000 names had been added/deleted and the process would continue till the last date for filing nominations: 29 August for the first phase, 7 September for the second, 13 September for the third, and 20 September for the fourth phase. For migrant Pandits special polling stations would be set up at six places in Jammu:

Gandhinagar, Janipur, Muthi, Chandrabhaga (Canal Road), Agricultural Complex (Gole Puli, Talaf Tilo) and Nagrota. There would be another in Jammu Division at the migrant camp in Udhampur. Finally, two special polling stations would be provided in Delhi at the Tis Hazari Courts and at the office of the resident commissioner, Jammu and Kashmir. For the two photographs submitted by the voter, the reimbursement ceiling was Rs. 15.

This press note also dealt with the de-clubbing of polling stations and the deputation of polling personnel from outside the state.

The dispersal of polling stations bunched together in the 1996 elections for security reasons, and the consequent increase of the total number of polling stations by 900 has been touched upon. A minuscule part of the addition was accounted for by auxiliary polling stations where the main polling stations had exceeded the limit of 1,500 voters per polling station. Another contributory factor was making sure that no voter had to walk for more than two kilometres.

To ensure the smooth functioning of EVMs during the polls and to promote confidence among candidates and voters, the commission would be deputing two out of the four officials of each polling party from Punjab and Uttar Pradesh—Doda being an exception—to Jammu and Kashmir. The Punjabis and Uttar Pradeshis were familiar with the EVM, having just done their own assembly elections in the first part of 2002.

In a word, the commission had not only fulfilled all the requests from the political parties, but gone beyond in two respects—special observers and voter slips.

The demand for 'international observers' persisted. As if 'international observers' were anything more than a collection of amateurs—not always well-intentioned—passing comments after the event. And as if our own were untrustworthy. I had just returned from a seminar in Cambridge—I have already referred to it—where I had been exposed at length to international observing in some of the Commonwealth countries, and it was mostly unflattering. So the mention of the subject touched a raw spot, and before I knew it I said, 'In this day and age, there is no question of the white man coming to observe what the native is doing . . . The white man does not determine what the coloured man does and whether he is doing it right or wrong.' (The last thing I expected after the announcement was a letter from Rashtriya Swayamsevak Sangh president K. Sudershan in which he appreciated the comment and called me a true patriot).

Rashtriya Swayamsevak Sangh
Head Office—Nagpur

4.8.2002 AD

To
Hon. J.M. Lyngdoh
Chief Election Commissioner
Govt of Bharat
New Delhi.

Dear Sir,

Please accept my congratulations for your very bold statement, appearing in yesterday's newspapers that 'the day of white man observing what the native does is long past, and again the Election Commission of India is competent enough to conduct free and fair elections and there is no need to think that the foreigners are better equipped to do the job'.

Only an intensely patriotic and courageous person can make such a statement. You have made us all proud by your brave statement.

Thanking you,

Yours sincerely,
K. Sudershan

Asked if the Election Commission would be better-placed to do a free and fair election under governor's rule, my reply was, 'If the governor turns out to be one-sided, he would be much worse than an elected government.'

The *Indian Express* was still determined to see the commission as the Government of India's toady. Despite the fact that, according to it, former law minister Ram Jethmalani, 'New Delhi's unofficial emissary with separatists', had called the announcement of the elections 'a hasty move'. The government was, from the paper's point of view, simultaneously pursuing another angle aimed at pressurizing groups yet unwilling to participate in the elections, by having the Election Commission announce elections without delay.

There were no questions on one of the most interesting aspects of the elections announced—the four-phasing. Not the number of phases per se, but the logic of the four phases. The four phases in chronological order were: (i) Baramulla, Kupwara, Poonch, Rajouri, Leh and Kargil (ii) Srinagar, Jammu and Badgam (iii) Anantnag, Pulwama, Udhampur and Kathua (iv) Doda.

There were security forces aplenty in Jammu and Kashmir but they were fully engaged with their normal duties. A lot more were required just to conduct the elections. Elections were a series of transparent pre-scheduled events, very easy to target for internal disrupters and Pakistan-inspired terrorists. They were even more fragile because only a fraction of the Central paramilitary forces (CPMF) required was available. So a phasing of the elections involving shifting of the same available forces from place to place within a timetable was inevitable.

The number of phases and sequencing depended on the following factors/principles: the strength of the Central paramilitary forces set aside exclusively for election duty; putting the more terrorism-beset districts towards the end and winding up with Doda, where de-induction or retrieval— because of terrain, extensiveness of area and concentration of militancy—would take twice as much time (a week) as anywhere else; every district, as a whole, would go to the polls on one single day; geographical proximity, compactness and nature of terrain were crucial considerations; the LoC districts had to be in the first stage because the Army, in great strength on the border, was there to give support; as far as possible there had to be an equitable distribution of work in terms of numbers of assembly constituencies and polling stations between the different phases.

The proposal of the state's director general of police— Rajouri, Poonch, Kupwara, Badgam in the first phase, Jammu, Baramulla, Leh and Kargil in the second, Udhampur, the Ramban segment of Doda district and Srinagar in the third, and the rest of Doda, Anantnag and Pulwama in the fourth phase—was at variance with some of the principles decided, and was summarily rejected.

The phasing announced on 2 August involved initiating elections on the LoC in the west, north and north-east and along Himachal in the east and then squeezing into Doda in south-central Jammu and Kashmir. The availability of CPMF and logistics dictated two phases between the first and last. In the first three phases difficult areas electorally were partly balanced by easier ones. Finally it met all the requirements. Including equity for the arrangement arrived at catered to 26 assembly constituencies and 2,265 polling stations in the first phase, 28 assembly constituencies and 2,160 polling stations in the second, 27 assembly constituencies and 2,114 polling stations in the third. This left a remainder of just 6 assembly constituencies and 534 polling stations in the fourth phase.

Interestingly, the first and fourth phases in the 1996 elections encompassed the same places as in 2002, but the second and third phases places then were reversed in order, in 2002.

*

There was a debriefing of the nine-member team to Gujarat on 5 and 6 August. It was decided as a measure of abundant caution that the full commission would also visit Gujarat to make its own assessment.

*

Instructions were issued on 6 August for computerizing electoral rolls in Hindi in the largely Hindi-speaking districts of Jammu, Udhampur and Kathua. In addition, rolls were to be computerized in Hindi for the districts of Poonch and Rajouri to enable the non-Urdu-knowing polling parties from Punjab to function efficiently.

On the same day, we also took measures to ease out a key Jammu and Kashmir state government functionary, having been told that false vigilance cases were being foisted on upright officers to scutch them and make them pliable.

On 7 August there was a meeting with Foreign Secretary

Kanwal Sibal on dealing with diplomats who wished to watch the Jammu and Kashmir elections. In the June press conference in Srinagar I had promised diplomats full access to the polling stations, and it was intended that though they could not and would not be recognized as official observers, they would be substituting for 'international observers'. Except that the commission would not be taking the kind of post-election report or comments that usually came to the country holding elections from officially recognized 'international observers'. And, of course, by the terms set out in the June press conferences in Srinagar and Jammu, the diplomats would be watching in their individual capacities.

The Ministry of External Affairs was more familiar with how to deal with diplomats. More importantly the people there knew all the accredited diplomats based in India. So the ministry had to be an interface between the commission and the diplomatic corps. The decisions in the meeting with Sibal, therefore, were: the Election Commission would provide passes for free access to accredited diplomats based in India; diplomats would route requests through the Ministry of External Affairs; the ministry would designate their focal point for the purpose [joint secretary (Iran, Pakistan and Afghanistan)]; the ministry would move for the diplomats' security and transport—helicopters to be made available at Srinagar and Jammu airports; diplomats to move in groups with group security, there not being enough resources to provide for separate security for each individual.

*

The full commission visited Ahmedabad and Vadodara in its 9 to 11 August tour of Gujarat. It used the successful methods of the nine-member team, utilized confidential sources for deciding where to go and announced the programme for the day just before starting out. The media not only appeared in unprecedented strength; it was dogged, persistent—it rose with us and figuratively went to bed with us—and unflaggingly enthusiastic. It attracted the people who had suffered and it slogged through all the dirty lanes with us. It shot and recorded continuously, and one could not breathe or sneeze or speak without being 'captured'. All intolerably suffocating. But it was providing useful information not forthcoming from the state administration. The experience broke a mental barrier. As a bureaucrat one had retired ever-wary of the media, but had always considered one's colleagues as more dependable than other people. Here things were just the other way round.

The commission went first to Ahmedabad and visited Gulmarg Society, Dr. Gandhi Ni Chali, Hukumsing Ni Chali, Bai Santok Ni Chali, Naroda Patia, Junador Bazar, Berhampura (Ghasyram Chali), Mariam Bibi Chali, Ambica Mill Ka Chapra, Kazmi, Delite, Tarana and Elite Apartments and Gupta Nagar. It also visited the Shah Alam Camp, Qureshi Jamat Hall, Mirzapur and Hugg House.

In-between it met the chief secretary, home secretary and director general of police and his hierarchy. The chief secretary was going to make an audio-visual presentation, but before that there was the usual proemial flattery which many bureaucrats today reserve for their 'political masters', as well as a smugness and make-believe that all was well with Gujarat. It was the media that was exaggerating things, as though to suggest we had been taken in and were wasting our time. In disgust I cut short the presentation and said we had not come to exchange pleasantries. From what we had seen the situation was far from normal, and we had been told that many of the accused in the communal riots had not been arrested, and were in fact threatening reprisals against the victims should they pursue the cases or depose against them. I then asked the chief secretary: had first information reports been registered against all culprits complained against, particularly VIPs? How many had been arrested/let out on bail? How many of those on bail had had their bail opposed by the government? How many had been charge-sheeted/were under final report? How many had been convicted/acquitted? Against how many of those acquitted had appeals been filed by the government? All this 'unnecessary' questioning disturbed the carefully structured symmetry of the meeting, and it suddenly disintegrated. The chief secretary was beyond his depth; the director general of police took over and dished out a lot of meaningless statistics. The home secretary made no more sense than the others. As though to save the prestige of Gujarat officialdom, the additional director general, R.B. Sree Kumar—he had had a distinguished stint with the Intelligence Bureau— spoke about reality. He said there was an undercurrent of fear and tension beneath the apparent normalcy which prevented interaction between the two communities. Though the moderates on both sides were trying to bring them together, the hawks were keeping them asunder. The new commissioner of police, K.R. Kaushik, agreed with him.

The commission met retired chief justices of different high courts, political parties, NGOs, organizations manning relief camps, social and cultural organizations . . . The BJP supporters, whatever else they might have said, all asked why we were hesitating with elections in Gujarat, when we were not doing so in Jammu and Kashmir.

The BJP tactic—the propaganda of 1:2 or Lyngdoh versus Krishna Murthy and Tandon—fetched high decibels to begin with, but by the evening the Gujarat government seemed to sense it had been had. There was complete solidarity in the commission with no evidence of a loose stitch anywhere. (However, when in Vadodara I told the print media I had colleagues who were probably better people than me, and everything ought not to be attributed to me—especially when we were a trio deciding things jointly—only UNI mentioned it.) The state government was also rattled by what the Election Commission had been able to see and hear for itself.

At Vadodara the district magistrate, who collected us from the airport and sat with me in the car that took me to the Circuit House, was evidently charged with seeing we got a better impression of the state administration there. If I didn't know about it, Vadodara was a respectable city of academics and institutions and therefore inherently above violence. This and an alert police administration confined casualties to the minimum. The presentation later by the police commissioner was on the same lines.

Unfortunately for them, the first place visited, Best Bakery, disproved their version. There, fifteen people were burnt alive and a young girl who had seen her relatives perish was taken to a lonely place to be raped. When confronted, the district magistrate tried to explain it away by saying the locality was on the outskirts of the city and therefore police help was slow in coming. The bakery on Dabhoi Road was in fact very much inside the city. It was then that I said they were a bunch of jokers—which was picked up by live TV coverage. It was a censorious comment from senior to junior, but since everything was bugged, what I had said was later thrown back at me by friend and foe.

The other areas visited were Hussaini Chowk, Raja

Rani Talav, Bachawada, Dhobi Talav, Baranapura, Noor Park, Maretha and Maneja villages. In one of the lanes somebody officious was obstructing our inquiry and thrusting the government's angle on us. When I asked him if he was an agent of the police, this also was telecast everywhere.

There were delegations similar to those in Ahmedabad but this time many more in favour of the BJP. None of them forgot to ask the familiar question—if elections in Jammu and Kashmir, why not in Gujarat?

Vadodara appeared to be even more damaging to the state government. The only way the BJP could get an early election in Gujarat—it appeared to them—was to put unbearable pressure on the commission. A case was registered in one of the smaller towns of Gujarat against all three election commissioners for disrespect to the national flag. (A small flag on a table in the conference hall of the Election Commission was shown upside down in TV coverage of the announcement of the Jammu and Kashmir elections on 2 August.) A pleader's notice from the obstructer whom I had asked if he was an agent of the police, was to follow. Not that they had not used pressure tactics earlier. To recall, Arun Jaitley on 19 July had hectored the Election Commission on the point that it was bound to conduct an early election on the dissolution of the Gujarat assembly; and before Venkaiah Naidu and he met the commission on 24 July, the 1:2 propaganda and an inspired leak that the commission would become a five-member body had been let loose. We agreed with the findings of the nine-member team.

*

On 13 August, the commission had a meeting with the chief electoral officers of Uttar Pradesh, Punjab and Jammu and

Kashmir, the Ministry of Home Affairs, the Department of Expenditure, the Ministry of Defence, the Department of Personnel, the divisional commissioners of Kashmir and Jammu divisions, and the secretary of finance, Jammu and Kashmir. This was on the movement of polling personnel from Uttar Pradesh and Punjab.

Where would the money come from? The representative of the Department of Expenditure guaranteed the funds and said he would write to the finance commissioners of Uttar Pradesh and Punjab. The cost of the airlifting of the poll personnel from Uttar Pradesh would be paid directly to the air force.

Joint secretary (Air), Ministry of Defence, said fourteen to fifteen sorties would be required for flying the poll personnel from Uttar Pradesh. It would take three to four days, and the airlifting would be from Lucknow and Hindon. The pulling-out operations would be concentrated in Avantipur airfield in the Valley. The return operation would need to be swift and efficient to minimize idle time for the aircraft and connected personnel. The type of aircraft used in and out of Kashmir would be the same. The onward airlift would commence from 7 September 2002 and the return airlift from 2 October. The poll personnel would return to the airfields from which they had been originally airlifted.

Decisions were on the following lines—

The personnel from Uttar Pradesh would be going to the Valley and their counterparts from Punjab to Jammu, as decided earlier. In 50 per cent of the polling stations in every assembly constituency, the presiding officer would be from either Uttar Pradesh or Punjab, and of the three other polling personnel, two would be from Jammu and Kashmir and the third from the state of the presiding officer. In the remaining 50 per cent of the polling stations, the presiding officer and one of the other polling officers would be from Jammu and Kashmir, and the remaining two polling officers from either Punjab or Uttar Pradesh. The chief electoral officers of Uttar Pradesh and Punjab would make up these pairs and assign to each a code number. For the onward airlift from Uttar Pradesh, the first to leave would be those who would be doing duty in Kupwara district, and they would be followed by those who had to go to Baramulla district.

Depending on where they were coming from, the Uttar Pradesh personnel would fly from either Lucknow or Hindon. The entire lot would be airlifted to Srinagar between 7 and 11 September. At Srinagar they would be bifurcated, one group going to Baramulla and another to Kupwara. In these districts they would be taken to their respective CPMF (Central Paramilitary Forces) camps where they would dine in the common mess. Lodging would be at the camp. This was also the venue where the poll personnel from outside the state were to be matched with their opposite numbers from the state as well as with the security personnel who would take them to the polling stations, do static duty for the poll, and bring back the polling party to the collection centre where the EVMs used in the polls would be deposited. The CPMF party would then escort the polling personnel to the camps from which they had started. The polling personnel would then move under escort to the CPMF camps in Srinagar and Badgam for the second phase, go through similar operations, and then proceed to Anantnag and Pulwama for the third phase, before returning home.

The Punjab personnel would be deployed in the districts of Rajouri, Poonch, Jammu, Udhampur and Kathua. The requirement of manpower for the first phase—Poonch and

Rajouri—would be considerably lower than that for the second or third phase. For Poonch and Rajouri only 1,600 persons would be required. They would be travelling by bus from Punjab—leaving on 11 September, via Jammu—to Poonch and Rajouri. After one day's halt at Jammu the same buses would take the polling parties to the CMPF camps in Rajouri and Poonch. From there onwards the polling parties would be combined with their Jammu and Kashmir counterparts and CMPF escorts in the same way as the UP polling parties going to Kupwara, and they would return in similar fashion having deposited the EVMs in the respective collection centres. They would repeat operations for the second and third phases. For the second phase there would be an additional 900 personnel moving in from Punjab four days before the polling date.

To avoid confusion the chief electoral officer, Jammu and Kashmir, would immediately intimate his counterparts in UP and Punjab the polling station locations in each district to match these with the polling personnel required. There would have to be a margin in terms of reserves. Also, for remote polling stations, taking two or three days to access, each polling party would consist of five persons instead of four.

Standard issues to the poll personnel would be decided by the chief electoral officers of Uttar Pradesh and Punjab after vetting by the chief electoral officer, Jammu and Kashmir. The commission recommended sleeping bags, medical kits and bullet-proof jackets.

The financial sheet showed: Rs. 34,000,000 to be advanced to each of the states of Uttar Pradesh and Punjab; the cost of airlift to be paid directly by the Ministry of Defence.

The chief electoral officer, Jammu and Kashmir, in

consultation with the director general police and the two divisional commissioners, was to calculate the expenditure of the Jammu and Kashmir government and pass it on to the principal secretary, finance, of the state for onward transmission to the Department of Expenditure, Government of India.

One aspect of the media policy vis-à-vis the elections had been decided at the Srinagar press conference in June: free access to accredited media, national and international. But would there be a role for government and government-controlled media agencies beyond disseminating information on EVMs and if so, how was one to use them? It had to be taken into account that overusing official channels would be counterproductive, the Kashmiris ever smelling a rat in every government effort and taking it as propaganda.

The proper function for them, given the sensitivity of the elections and the distinct possibility of sabotage by militants in the garb of journalists, was to select journalists who had some form of accreditation to a media group. The Press Information Bureau and state publicity department would then issue the passes.

This was formalized in a commission meeting with the principal information officer on 13 August. Decisions on other items included: PIB coordinating all official press releases of the commission through their regional networks; giving passes to foreign correspondents without PIB accreditation, after they had obtained visas from MEA and applied for passes through PIB; PIB offices in Srinagar and Jammu obtaining photographs depicting key events and disseminating them; Doordarshan and All India Radio preparing, on behalf of the Election Commission, short programmes on why it was necessary to vote.

With the operation of the Code of Conduct, the shifting

of questionable officers had begun. On 14 August the state government was also directed to transfer all election-related officers who had served in their home districts for four years or more.

On 15 August, making an Independence Day speech* at the Red Fort, Vajpayee again promised free and fair elections:

> The process of peace and democracy has now arrived at a decisive turn in Jammu and Kashmir, which has been grappling with terrorism.
>
> Elections are going to take place in the state. The dates have already been announced.
>
> I am confident that these elections will be fully free and fair. No one need have any doubts on this score.
>
> I appeal to the people of Jammu, Kashmir, and Ladakh, as also to their representatives to participate actively and in large numbers in the elections and thereby demolish the motivated propaganda being conducted from across the border. No one will be allowed to create disturbances in the elections in Jammu and Kashmir. All the designs to create an atmosphere of fear will be frustrated.

Though the prime minister's guarantee of free and fair elections in Jammu and Kashmir was again embarrassing to the Commission, Vajpayee's patent sincerity showed through and we realized this was why the Government of India had so easily agreed to pay for the expenses of the polling parties from Uttar Pradesh and Punjab.

The Times of India (Delhi), 30 September 2002

23

Mid-August to 10 October 2002—
Credibility and Confidence Building;
Voting and Results

The very next day the commission issued an order on the Gujarat elections. The reader is already privy to the views of the nine-member team and of the full Election Commission thereafter. More interesting are the arguments—summarized below—regarding the constitutional position on Article 174, and the imperative of free and fair elections.

The commission had always (and consistently) held that the six months in Article 174(1) of the Constitution applied not only to a legislative assembly in existence but to one that had been prematurely dissolved, and where the President had not taken over the administration of the state under Article 356, elections to constitute a new legislative assembly had always been held within such time as enabled a new assembly to meet within six months of the last date of the last session of the dissolved assembly. If this interpretation were not accepted, there could be wide gaps between two Houses of a legislature, and this would be an abuse of democracy. All the more so because there was no provision in the Constitution, or in any law in force, prescribing a period during which an election was to be held to constitute a new House on the dissolution of the old one. It would be much worse with more than six months between one Lok Sabha and another.

The commission's interpretation was fortified by the view taken by the President and Parliament on the provisions of Article 174(1) whenever there was an imposition of President's rule in a state under Article 356. Every time the legislative assembly of a state had been dissolved by the President under Article 356, the provisions of Article 174(1) had invariably been expressly suspended in the Presidential proclamation, and this had been approved by Parliament during the operation of the proclamation.

But was the commission, whatever be the circumstances, obliged to hold the Gujarat elections within the period remaining of the six months from the date of the last sitting of the dissolved assembly? From the Commission's point of view the answer was 'no'. Article 324, which was not subject to the provisions of any other article, vested the superintendence, direction and control of the preparation of electoral rolls for, and conduct of, elections to Parliament and the state legislatures, in the Election Commission. Elections in the context of democratic institutions could only mean free and fair elections. Free and fair elections were a requirement not only of Supreme Court orders, but of the 1948 Universal Declaration of Human Rights and Declaration of the Inter-Parliamentary Council.

If free and fair elections could not be held at any point in time because of some extraordinary circumstances, Article 174(1) would have to yield to Article 324. And this was a situation which had not been contemplated under the Constitution. In the commission's view, non-observance of the provisions of Article 174(1) would mean the government of the state could not be carried on in accordance with the provisions of the Constitution within the meaning of Article 356—and therefore President's rule would have to follow.

It was for the Election Commission alone to decide when free and fair elections could be held. The Supreme Court had upheld this. The Constitution was aware that President's rule in a state could be extended by Parliament beyond one year from the date of imposition only on a commission certificate that a general election to its legislative assembly was not possible. Section 15 of the Representation of the People Act, 1951, also said that the governor should call upon the assembly constituencies to elect a new assembly on such date or dates as recommended by the Election Commission.

The order referred to the visits of the nine-member team and full commission and the findings already referred to. It also contained the commission's directions. These were: a house-to-house special revision of electoral rolls in all the twenty generally riot-affected districts, and in the villages of other districts similarly affected; names of dead people and of those who had shifted elsewhere in the state to be deleted from the electoral rolls of the places where they had been ordinarily resident; on the other hand, the names of those who had shifted to be included in the electoral rolls in their new places; the rolls to be finally published by 15 October 2002, every effort being made to trace electors who had temporarily migrated to other states (rough estimates indicated there were 20,000 such electors. The effort was to take the form of wide publicity—on the special revision of electoral rolls—in the states of Maharashtra, Madhya Pradesh, Rajasthan, Uttar Pradesh and Bihar. There was to be no deletion of the names of such voters merely on the ground of temporary absence from Gujarat); the identity cards programme would be recommenced from 1 October 2002 in the areas affected by the riots, as by then the house-to-house verification of electors would have been over. (In the five districts not affected by riots the programme could begin right away.) The order also required that the guilty be arrested; physical obstructions to deny access of riot-affected people to their destroyed homes be removed; the CPMF be inducted in large numbers in affected areas, and that permanent pickets be set up; shortcomings in the relief and rehabilitation measures be removed, and restoration and rehabilitation work be completed to restore the confidence of affected people; and officers who performed their duties fearlessly be restored to their original postings.

The commission would consider a suitable election schedule in November/December.

On 18 August the Union government, unhappy with the 16 August order of the Election Commission, made a presidential reference to the Supreme Court instead of appealing to the court.

*

Nothing established the Election Commission's independence more than the Gujarat order of 16 August, and it had to thank Arun Jaitley and Narendra Modi for dissolving the Gujarat assembly prematurely, and bringing the Gujarat and Jammu and Kashmir elections within a common public focus. The proof of this was reflected in the commission's experience during its third trip to Jammu and Kashmir (18–20 August). It began at Palam airport. Between the terminal and the plane a Kashmiri lady smiled and asked if I remembered her. The face was familiar, it was Mrs Azad (her husband, Ghulam Nabi Azad, had been my minister in the Tourism Department, Government of India) and she warmly congratulated the Election Commission for its stand on Gujarat. As I passed my jacket to an air-hostess to be stowed away, she playfully asked me if she could wear it. At the Srinagar end, state government functionaries applauded the commission and politicians began to take their elections more seriously.

In the meeting with the Unified Command in Srinagar, the generals individually congratulated us for an 'excellent' job in Gujarat, though generals in India did not normally vouchsafe complimentary remarks to civilians. It was this that gave me hope the army would be on its best behaviour at the elections.

The meeting was a comprehensive forum—military, civil and police—and I made only two points. Contrary to all previous elections in the state the Election Commission would be stricter than it had been even in the elections in Uttar Pradesh and Bihar. The army and police would not be allowed to force anyone to vote. They—excluding the police on poll duty—would merely dominate the areas and sanitize them, and create a conducive atmosphere for voting.

No one had a keener nose for potential trouble than Sayan, and no one was more forthright and more adept at problem-solving than Malhi, the state chief secretary. In the discussions with the chief secretary and director general of police, the commission concentrated on securing some sort of control on the 'STF'/'SOG' and 'SPOs', the kind of forces complained against by political parties in June. It was decided that the 'STF'/'SOG' would not conduct operations on their own but only in conjunction with the CRPF/BSF/ army; any surrendered militant in any uniformed service or functioning as a special police officer would be lodged in an army camp and not allowed to take part in any operation till the end of the elections; movements by deputation between the Jammu and Kashmir police and the 'STF'/'SOG' would be frozen till elections were over; the 'STF'/'SOG' would not be put on static duty in the inner or outer security ring of any polling station; the additional director general in charge of law and order and security would be divested of security; a panel of three suitable officers would be sent to the commission for appointment as additional director general, Security; the chief electoral officer would be associated with the state police deployment plan, and the district election officers or deputy commissioners would have to countersign the district police deployment plans; all observers would be provided adequate security, including bullet-proof cars, by diversion from local officers if necessary; all candidates in any constituency were to be given equal security.

In Jammu, there was a meeting with the deputy commissioners of Jammu Division, Jammu being even further behind Srinagar than before in its preparedness for the elections. The deputy commissioner of Jammu exaggerated the defects in his own electoral rolls, and at one point I was determined that he should be changed. On closer scrutiny, the Jammu electoral rolls were neither better nor worse than those of the other districts.

An important element of imparting transparency in the electoral process and getting the electoral rolls as accurate as possible was displaying them in public places, as soon as they had been computerized. We drove down the Sialkot road to Miran Sahib High School. The rolls had been put up in one polling station that very morning, but not yet in another. We also visited the R.S. Pura Tehsil office. (Sialkot is just a few kilometres away and this was one of the routes by which Jammu and Kashmir could be accessed in the old days. The other was from Rawalpindi.) The electoral rolls were still being corrected in the tehsil office.

We then called at the Purkhu and Muthi Kashmiri migrant camps off the Rajouri road to review arrangements for separate polling stations for camp inmates. By the time we came to Muthi it was clear that the voting facility had been almost entirely forgotten, the Pandits being so involved with their woes and seeing everybody else as sadists and tormentors. And then there was the familiar question—if you could have elections in Jammu and Kashmir with all the Pandits killed and evicted in the Valley, what was so unusual about Muslims suffering the same way in Gujarat, that one had to delay elections there? The only advantage from these visits was that we were able to tie up the polling arrangements with the camp commandant.

Since the immigrant Pandits were unwilling to go back to the Valley, and yet were inseparably attached to their native places to the extent that they were not agreeable to being enrolled where they were, the commission had to resort to a strategem. They would continue to be on the old rolls in the Valley, but they would be allowed to vote wherever they were. All they had to do was to make a request and an indication would be made in their original electoral rolls that they would be voting in Jammu or Delhi or wherever. This would also prevent impersonation in the relevant Valley polling stations. Fortunately Section 36(A) of the Jammu and Kashmir Representation of the People Act, 1957, allowed polling stations outside the territorial limits of constituencies to safeguard the franchise of 'such class of persons who for reasons of security are not in a position to give their votes in the polling stations provided under section 36'.

According to the relief commissioner, Jammu and

Kashmir, 34,379 Kashmiri migrant families were registered with him. In addition, 19,165 families were registered with the divisional commissioner, Delhi.

*

Narendra Modi reacted to the Election Commission's 16 August orders on 20 August. It was a personal attack saying I was biased, that I had been to only two cities and brought out an order of forty pages. 'How can the mood of 5 crore people be gauged like that?' He added, 'Has Lyngdoh come from Italy? Is he a relation of Sonia Gandhi? They sometimes meet in the church, so there have to be ties. His interest lies with the minorities, and thus against the Hindus.' He was just adding to the commission's credibility in Jammu and Kashmir.

*

Diplomats in large numbers started descending on the commission in the third week of August. Basically they wanted to ascertain the facilities/logistical arrangements. The most prominent among them were from the US, UK, Canada, Japan, Sweden, Germany, France and the European Union.

The commission was then closely interacting with the Ministry of External Affairs to work out access, security and transport for diplomats. The ministry secured approval from the Ministry of Defence for two helicopters to be stationed in Srinagar for each of the three phases of polling in Srinagar Division. One helicopter was to be made available in Jammu for the first phase of the elections in Jammu Division, that is, for Poonch and Rajouri. Security and vehicles for movement to the polling stations were to be provided by the state government. So too accommodation, but on payment. Only group security was to be provided, the size of each group and its itinerary being left to the diplomats to decide. Passes for one phase could be used for a subsequent one, but they were not transferable. Altogether thirty passes to diplomats from sixteen countries and the European Commission were issued. The home commissioner, Jammu and Kashmir, and the divisional commissioners of Srinagar and Jammu were the coordinators for the entire operation. One of the divisional commissioners, Parvez Dewan, author of *The Names of Allah*, was specially mentioned in connection with the commendable work done.

A commission letter of 22 August says that two of the polling personnel in each polling station in Doda would be from Jammu region. But the conditions were that they should not have worked or been domiciled in the assembly constituencies in which they were being deputed.

Special observers had begun to systematically scrutinize the backgrounds of senior officers in the field, and on 22 August, the senior superintendent of police, Jammu, was transferred.

*

On 23 August, in an interview with Rajdeep Sardesai and Arnab Goswami of NDTV for Star News, I at last took the pleasure of referring to Modi's preposterous personal remarks as 'menial gossip' (which seems later to have been closely examined in Ahmedabad as a possible allusion to untouchables). Besides, he didn't seem to have heard of atheism.

By our Gujarat experience, the electronic media had

proved itself superior to the print media in covering fluid events—it had the advantages of immediacy and basic veracity. That is, a compulsive coherence of picture, sound and presentation as well as of outreach against a lot of subjective reportage later rectified in editorial columns. And the Indian electronic media had not only matured but literally displaced its foreign counterpart. So we had to be sure it would be in strength in Jammu and Kashmir, doing the elections. Zee TV, NDTV for Star News, ANI and Aaj Tak turned up at the commission on 23 August. Zee and ANI said they were going to have a special election coverage, but the other two merely smiled—the media had got to a stage where it was often seen to be more potent than nation-states themselves, never mind governments and election commissions—and they were pleased to keep their doings to themselves. It was enough that over Gujarat the commission and media had developed a professional respect for each other.

The commission's letter to the chief secretary, Jammu and Kashmir, confirming that the Special Task Force/Special Operation Group were not to conduct operations on their own, but only with the paramilitary forces and the army, was also dated 23 August.

The letter requiring special police officers to be immured in security camps was issued on 29 August. What is important is that in our previous visit to the state, we were either 'led up the garden path' or went that way on our own, thinking that the 'STF'/'SOG' and 'SPOs' were under the official rubric security. We even had M.K. Mohanty posted as additional director general, Security, before he told us he still had nothing to do with the 'STF'/'SOG'. It was he who indicated that they were under the inspectors general of Srinagar and Jammu. So the 29 August letter also required these two inspectors general to report directly to the director general of police, and not the additional director general, Law and Order. This is an example of how tricky it was to deal with the Jammu and Kashmir police.

On 2 September a letter from the commission to the Ministry of External Affairs requested publicity outside the country on special initiatives for the Jammu and Kashmir elections. The idea was to elaborate all measures taken to establish complete transparency with the hope that this would build a positive international opinion on the fairness of the entire electoral exercise.

A commission letter of 5 September confirmed that all observers were to be given adequate security and all candidates in any constituency given equal security.

The Model Code of Conduct in Jammu and Kashmir had, for the first time, to be very strictly enforced in 2002. It was most apt to be infringed by the state government in respect of the use of its own aircraft. On 5 September the commission directed the Director General, Civil Aviation, not to allow any flight by state-owned aircraft unless the chief secretary of Jammu and Kashmir gave a signed certificate saying that it had the clearance of the Election Commission of India. A state helicopter had admittedly been used on 7 August by the chief minister for political meetings at Sunder Pani and Nuasera in Rajouri District under cover of a looser dispensation of 1998 in which the commission had allowed state helicopters to be used by Jammu and Kashmir politicians on payment on a first-come first-served basis. But curiously, the first infringement of the code was by a Bahujan Samaj Party minister from Uttar Pradesh who had used one of his state government planes to drop BSP supremo Kanshi Ram in Jammu. The minister had to pay for the entire cost of the use of the aircraft.

Came September, and the commission visited Jammu
and Kashmir again—6th and 7th.

The Jet Airways plane had barely come to a stop when
we transferred to one of the three state government Bell
helicopters—it was supposed to have a flying ceiling of
20,000 ft, but the manufacturers were not sure and expected
a report from the pilots after it had been pushed to its
limits—and made for Poonch. The late Group Captain
Kahlon, who had put a chopper down on many a mountain
in the most inclement weather but very sadly crashed and
died taxiing well-heeled but slothful pilgrims to Amarnath,
was still fuming, 'black cats' accompanying Sonia Gandhi
having directed him to remove his helicopter from the
airport apron and he having responded by threatening to
shoot them. One was amazed at the sheer number of first-
quality brick kilns in the Srinagar suburbs. (The building
trade was busier in Srinagar than anywhere else in India—
houses with the interiors of Swiss chalets courtesy the
thriving militancy-cum-terrorism industry.) There were great
squirls of gold, brown and green paddy and long sharp
ridges that one intersected, occasionally lurched by a draught
along a valley between high hills freshly powdered with
snow. As one got nearer to Poonch the flat mud-roofed
houses below seemed indistinguishable from bunkers. Poonch
town presented itself as a hollow overlooked by Pakistan-
occupied Kashmir—two-thirds of old Poonch district is on
the other side. At the helipad a white dog not only refused
to budge as we came in to land but actually welcomed
us.

In the meeting with the deputy commissioner and the
superintendent of police our main concern was about polling
stations very near the line of control and susceptible to

Pakistani shelling, as well as those in militant-infested areas subject to blasting by mines or IEDs. Two alternative courses of action were indicated. The first for the armed forces to take these over five to six days before the poll and to sanitize them. Or the polling stations could be shifted hundreds of metres away from their permanent structures and located in tents. There were also some areas where armed road opening parties would have to force passage through militant areas three to four days before the polling and retain it.

Airborne again, one flew up the valley of the Betar—then lush with paddy—over Surankote, worth 7,000–8,000 people, prosperous with remittances from the Gulf and almost unbearably militant. The other side of Surankote, as though to give it cover, the enemy infested the sombre hills and fired their artillery freely over the line of control. Short of Rajouri was another settlement but much bigger—Mendhar with a population of 22,000. The Rajouri helipad was in the shadow of a five-hundred-year-old hilltop fortress.

The meeting with the deputy commissioner and superintendent of police did not throw up any peculiar local problems. But Rajouri and Poonch were going to be in the first phase of the elections, and we had gone there essentially to gauge their preparedness.

We took off again at 5.45 p.m. and discovered the clear sunny air had curdled. The path to Srinagar was blocked by dense cumulus, high hills and invisibility. So we turned towards Jammu and unwound from cloud and mountain heights only as we approached the Chenab. Relieved, one realized how vital skill, instinct and experience counted toward staying alive, flying in those parts.

We choppered to Srinagar the following morning overlooking Vaishno Devi temple, birds on the wing, extravagant grasslands, and after parting the Shivaliks and the Pir Panjal range—settlements in the Valley like dumps of empty tin cans and ripened paddy Gauguin masterpieces. Then followed in quick succession the Rambiar river, plateaux of apple cultivation, Avantipur airport, the Jhelum, brick kilns, the Cantonment, Oberoi Palace Hotel, Dal Lake and the helipad by Group Captain Kahlon's residence. Group Captain Kahlon lived in a pretty cottage then meditating impeccable lawns and seasonal flowers in decline but still besotting the bees.

In the meeting with the chief secretary and DGP our instructions on polling stations vulnerable to shelling across the LoC and IED explosions were iterated. It was anticipated that some diplomats would be needing bullet-proof vehicles, and after some hesitation it was decided that the vehicles—obviously in short supply—would be temporarily squeezed out of the possession of officers not in dire need of them. This was the last meeting before the elections, and security arrangements outside polling stations had to be hammered out. The decision was that the Central paramilitary forces would be doing static duty outside the polling stations in two concentric rings. The frisking of voters would be done by the state police, women special police officers frisking women voters.

We also visited a BSF camp near the airport to meet polling parties from Uttar Pradesh. The camp was well-appointed, but the few UP teachers left behind were caught in teething problems. Their spokesman was not happy that most of the party had dispersed to their respective areas of duty, and that no space had been assigned to him to relax while waiting for his own assignment. An adroit turn of conversation, however, immediately elicited an unambiguous averment of loyalty to the country and of dedication to the national duty of doing elections in the state.

K.J. Rao was to be the resident representative of the commission during the elections. On 8 September he was in Srinagar assessing the situation. Like most of us, he found officers praising Farooq Abdullah and predicting his return to power. At Kupwara and Baramulla he met the deputy commissioners, senior superintendents of police, returning officers and assistant returning officers, and made it clear that no one was to be forced to vote.

Written instructions to the chief secretary on the sanitization of polling stations near the LoC subject to shelling and others vulnerable to IED explosions were dispatched on 9 September.

On 11 September Mushtaq Ahmed Lone, National Conference candidate of Lolab assembly constituency, Kupwara district, and then minister of law, was gunned down by unidentified killers. The poll for this constituency was therefore countermanded and rescheduled for 8 October.

A commission order dated 10 September recognized that a substantial percentage of voters had been issued voter identity cards but since most of them had not, those without cards would be allowed to establish their identity on the basis of any one of twenty-one alternative documents—such as voters' slips, passports, ration cards and student identity cards.

Unlike the diplomats, the media started stirring only in September. Till the day of the first phase of the polls on 16 September there was a steady stream of requests for passes. One journalist from *Gulf News* turned up on the 14th without the requisite permission from the Ministry of External Affairs on his visa. At the end of some strenuous efforts all permits were obtained, and he was despatched well in time for the first phase of the elections.

Passes for local journalists were to be issued by the chief electoral officer from Srinagar. Rajouri and Poonch were going to the polls on 16 September, yet journalists from the two districts had not been given their passes even on the 14th. There were frenetic calls from the observers and deputy commissioners and passes issued by the commission were airlifted to the two districts by arrangement with the resident commissioner, Jammu and Kashmir, in Delhi and distributed through the divisional commissioner and deputy commissioners. For covering remote areas deputy commissioners were authorized to issue permits on their own.

A media facilitation centre was set up in Srinagar with phone and fax facilities. The chief electoral officer was responsible for daily press briefings and he—Pramod Jain—stuck to his task admirably.

At the commission, Ajay Jha liaised with media persons, sorted out the nitty-gritty of press relations (he had also dealt with the diplomats), issued passes and organized special briefings for select media persons with Sayan Chatterjee and me, among them Amy Waldeman of the *New York Times* and Myra McDonald, chief of Reuters. He was characteristically suave, courteous, patient and efficient. And there were no glitches anywhere.

A commission instruction of 13 September prescribed polling time as 7 a.m. to 4 p.m.

Polling was expected to be comparatively low in Srinagar, and political opportunism saw that migrant Pandits' postal ballots could be a deciding factor in many constituencies. When opposition parties alleged gross misuse of the scheme, Rao checked the postal ballot papers in Jammu on 14 September. He found that while there had been few applications for Baramulla and Kupwara districts in the first phase, there were 21,000 and 27 applications for Srinagar and Badgam districts respectively. The application forms were mostly questionable. Many were attested by the same officer, and in some cases attestation had been done by officers of Udhampur and of the neighbouring state of Himachal Pradesh. Many of the forms had been filled in the same handwriting, and signatures attributed to the same attesting officers varied.

Checking at the office of the executive engineer, PWD, Jammu, disclosed that there was no such officer as Assistant Engineer in charge, Store, Subdivision, Water Supply, Master Plan—one of the functionaries shown to have attested a whole lot of forms.

Inquiries in Udhampur indicated that the signatures of the attesting officers had been forged, that is, of the headmaster, Government High School, Barmeen, zonal education officer, Chenani and apiculture development assistant, Department of Agriculture, Katra, Udhampur. And a whole lot of forms carried 'care of' addresses of shops.

In respect of Habbakadal assembly constituency alone, 3,535 forms had been attested by only seventeen officers.

Fortunately, most of the applications were rejected by the assistant returning officer. But if Rao had not been so thorough in his inquiry, poll results in the Valley and therefore in the state as a whole would have been just that much different as would have mattered.

Rao's second visit to the Valley was on 15 September. He received complaints that personnel of the Agriculture Department—the agriculture minister himself being a candidate there—had been deployed on polling duty in Kupwara district. After confirmation, he got them replaced.

In the first phase of polling media coverage in Kupwara

district was focused on the large voter turnout, particularly in Handwara, where a rebel People Conference candidate was contesting, and Uri, which sits on the international border. The TV footage showed large crowds gathered in front of polling stations, in festive mood. There were critical comments on many people turning up after 4 p.m. but not being allowed to vote. Polling hours had been changed from 8 a.m. to 5 p.m. to 7 a.m. to 4 p.m., but the announcement of the change at the local level had been delayed.

In Baramulla district, particularly in Baramulla town and Sopore where the Hurriyat boycott of the elections was most effective, the media fastened on the low voter turnout and alleged voter-hustling by security forces. Barkha Dutt of NDTV–Star News cited examples which, on verification, did not substantiate the allegations. The channel subsequently corrected that part of the coverage.

In Poonch and Rajouri much of the TV footage was on the fate of polling stations along the border which were subjected to continuous shelling. Ajay Shukla of NDTV–Star News showed voters defying the shelling in many places.

The overall voting percentage was 47.25. This did not include Ladakh where two independent candidates were elected unopposed.

Heavy shelling from across the border created enough chaos for electoral malpractices in six polling stations in 85-Surankote and 86-Mendhar assembly constituencies. Repoll in these constituencies took place on 1 October.

On the night before the elections there were several violent incidents, but no damage was done. On the day of polling, however, a constable was shot by terrorists.

The third phase of the elections was to include Anantnag and Pulwama, the best apple country, the heart of Kashmiri culture, a densely populated and electorally important part of the Valley (sixteen seats), but also the epicentre of militancy. (Locally Anantnag is known as Islamabad.) The commission flew into Anantnag and Pulwama on the 19th afternoon. The helicopter was little above tree-level and one often marvelled that one had cleared an orchard on a bump in the plateau. Some of the apple trees were visibly quite dead and needed replacement. Over the downs was the iterated wonder of fat ripened paddy, in high lattitudes and at over four thousand feet above sea level—some of it harvested and in stooks. Many of the rooftops were rouged with drying chili.

There were meetings with the deputy commissioner, SSP, commandant, BSF and local brigadier in Anantnag, and deputy commissioner, SSP and commandant, BSF at Pulwama. While the two districts were prepared electorally, their deputy commissioners were a trifle too innocent about the kind of threats to the elections posed by militants. One has mentioned the state government's written denial through the Ministry of Home Affairs of the existence of a police force called the 'NDF'. In the meeting in Anantnag, however, one of the police officers blurted out that such a force had indeed been raised, and that it had consisted of surrendered militants on antagonistic terms with other ex-militants associated with 'STF'/'SOG' operations. The force had been disbanded in March 2002.

We visited two BSF camps and met polling personnel from Uttar Pradesh. The camps were inside the town, but in very salubrious surroundings. One was in an affluent school with gardens and playing fields. So the UP personnel were quite happy. All problems about food had been left far behind and in any case after excitingly hostile conditions in Kupwara and Baramulla, they were quite seasoned and battle-hardened. Compared to the Kashmiris, they were smaller and quite clearly less prosperous, but their Urdu was infinitely superior, and when it came to hill-climbing they were as tenacious and enduring as the best among their hosts. In fact the Kashmiris had a sneaking admiration for them.

At Srinagar, at the meeting with the chief secretary, DGP and major general (GOC Pulwama), the commission wanted the deputy commissioners of Anantnag and Pulwama to be changed. But with ten days left for the third phase polls, the chief secretary persuaded us not to insist on a change. On condition, of course, that the divisional commissioner and DIG of Srinagar would camp in Anantnag and effectively take over the law and order responsibility for the two districts. For Lolab constituency—where elections had to be countermanded because of the murder of the National Conference candidate, half the members of the polling party were to be from Uttar Pradesh. In addition, other Uttar Pradesh personnel would be persuaded to do extra duty in the polling stations of Doda for which they would be paid an additional ten thousand rupees each. It was also decided to send back the Railway Protection Force (RPF) in disgrace for having run away and left candidate Abdur Rehman Sheikh near Gorihakhar village in Handwara in Kupwara district, to be killed by militants. The home ministry were to be requested for a proper substitute force, not another sub-standard one.

K.J. Rao's third visit to Srinagar was on 22 September, a day ahead of the second phase involving Srinagar and Badgam districts in the Valley. He visited one of the distribution centres—that is, a place from where election material is distributed—Atma Ram College, at around 3 p.m. The car in which he, the deputy commissioner and

SSP travelled was stopped at the main entrance and thoroughly checked, and security seemed quite satisfactory. Distribution work was tardy, but Rao gingered it up. He left for the CEO's office, found that most of the staff had left by 5 p.m. on the pretext that the city was tense and anything could happen anytime. At 5.30 p.m. a peon requested that he be allowed to close the office. From there to the guest house Rao saw that the shops were closed and the traffic virtually non-existent.

At 9 p.m. the deputy commissioner, Srinagar, rang him up to say that two militants had entered a house adjacent to Atma Ram College, but that fortunately all the polling material, including EVMs, had been removed to a safer place. Rao wanted to visit the area again, but was dissuaded for security reasons; however, the deputy commissioner promised to keep in touch. Rao rang up the commission and took permission for stocking the election material in a building not far from the college.

At 11 p.m., the deputy commissioner phoned him again saying security forces had started flushing out the two terrorists who had captured the building next to Atma Ram College, and also taken two policemen as hostages.

At 11.30 p.m., Rao switched on his TV and saw a live telecast—on Zee News—of the operation. Rao wondered how a private channel could be so conveniently at the scene of what ought to have been a covert police operation. He asked Deputy Commissioner Abdul Hamid who told him the operation was being conducted by the IGP, Srinagar, and that this was entirely within the jurisdiction of the police. Rao subsequently learnt that the policemen held hostage had escaped and that the police would blast the captured building.

The following morning (polling day) at 8 a.m. Rao went

to the spot—the media were already there in full force—and met the IG, Srinagar, who said the operation would be over in an hour or so. It was not and continued for hours together. Rao went to the nearby polling station which also had been shifted, and found that by 8.30 a.m. not a vote had been cast. Polling was dull in other polling stations as well—in fact throughout the day.

The live coverage had shaken the sense of security of the voter and lowered the polling percentage in Srinagar, and the police were squarely responsible for it. The general feeling was that a low turnout would benefit the ruling party, its committed voters voting anyway. The question as to whether it was a put-up job has remained unanswered.

The media coverage, especially Zee News—was initially on the police–militants encounter in Srinagar city. It then swung to empty polling stations in Srinagar and contrasting heavy polling in Badgam and Gandharbal. It also showed extremely low Kashmiri migrant turnout in Delhi as against a substantially high turnout in Jammu. Here the main reporters were Barkha Dutt and Vikram Chandra of NDTV–Star News from Srinagar.

The average polling percentage was 40.6.

Repoll was done in two polling stations of 27-Badgam constituency of Badgam district and one polling station of 71-Gandhinagar constituency of Jammu district. This was because of electoral malpractices.

The Srinagar polls over, Rao left for Pulwama and Anantnag on the 25th morning. At Pulwama he met the district election officer (deputy commissioner) and the senior superintendent of police, and then the returning officers and assistant returning officers. He also saw representatives of political parties.

He then drove to Anantnag and went straight to the

guest house conference hall, assuming the meeting with the returning officers and assistant returning officers had been kept there. There was no civilian in that room and Rao was surprised to find it was on the contrary full of police officers in uniform. He made his excuses and left, only to be overtaken by the district election officer (deputy commissioner) and taken to another room where the returning officers and assistant returning officers were seated. When Rao asked the deputy commissioner why the conference hall was not available he was told that the director general of police and inspector general of police were reviewing security arrangements for the third phase of the elections due in Pulwama and Anantnag districts. Even though the commission had issued specific instructions that security arrangements in the districts were to be approved by the deputy commissioners, it did not then occur to Rao to ask himself why therefore this meeting was being confined to the police. When it came to lunch, the deputy commissioner came to Rao's room and told him the director general of police would like Rao to join him and the other police officers at the table.

The DGP and IGP told him they had discussed the deployment of forces and other matters. The DGP asked him whether he was travelling in a bullet-proof car and Rao replied that he had been served very well by an ordinary car. The solicitude was genuine, for Rao found he had been provided a bullet-proof car the following day. He chose not to use it as he felt suffocated in it.

Following the completion of the second phase the commission made the last visit to the state—to Doda, which would see the fourth and last phase. During the Indian Airlines flight to Jammu of 27 September we were astonished to find news reports in the important dailies—the *Hindu*, the *Tribune*, the *Indian Express*, the *Hindustan Times*, the *National Herald* and the *Economic Times* carrying a threat by the Peoples Democratic Party to pull out of the polls because the police were determined to rig the rest of the elections in favour of the ruling party in the state. According to the *Hindu*, the Peoples Democratic Party vice-president, Muzaffar Hussain Beig, said the police were behaving like 'card-holders of the NC'. Beig alleged 'the state police chief (A.K. Suri) had conducted a meeting of police officers in south Kashmir and told them to "forget the directions of Election Commission and help the National Conference", the report continued.

'Mr Beig said that though the first two phases of elections were conducted satisfactorily, the police have started behaving differently.

'The Electronic Voting Machines (EVMs) were not safe and were being protected by the Central forces, which were under the home ministry, he said, adding "the Election Commission should ensure that these are really protected".

'Beig urged the "Election Commission to restrain the security forces and the police and ensure protection of the EVMs, and if it is not done we may have to withdraw from the elections".'

The *National Herald* carried a quotation from Peoples Democratic Party president Mufti Mohammad Sayeed, which alleged that the National Conference government was using 'State police and renegades to ensure victory of the ruling party nominees in South Kashmir and Doda district'.

We used a chopper from Jammu to Doda and saw that the railway line to Srinagar had been built up to Udhampur, tunnels included, and only the bridges were missing. As one found the Chenab and pursued it upstream, there were round, sculpted stone hills. One also saw the alternate route to the Valley from Kishtwar.

At the meeting with the chief secretary, director general of police, deputy commissioner and senior superintendent of police, Doda, a review of the poll arrangements indicated that we were dealing with a very competent district administration.

On the way back to Jammu we overflew the Baghliar Hydel Project, under construction on the Chenab.

At Jammu the meeting with the chief secretary, director general of police, army and BSF commanders was followed by dinner. At dinner I remember having drawn everyone's attention to the newspaper reports of the day on the DGP and 'STF'/'SOG', and telling the DGP that if this was true, it was unacceptable and contrary to everyone's, including the army's, attempt at doing good elections in the state. What surprised the commission were requests that we allow Farooq Abdullah to use the state helicopter freely, for security reasons. Many officers could not understand why this kind of privilege should be confined to the prime minister.

On verification from its own sources the commission decided to tie the 'SOG'/'STF' down. It took no chances, and the following day issued written instructions to the chief secretary from Jammu itself: the 'SOG'/'STF' in Pulwama and Anantnag would be confined to police lines; any operation involving the 'STF'/'SOG' would need the joint clearance of the SSP, deputy commissioner and special observer of the district concerned; any independent superintendent of police/deputy superintendent of police in charge of 'SOG' operations would report to the senior superintendent of police in respect of 'SOG' matters; the commission's consultant, K.J. Rao, would enforce implementation of the instructions.

The following day newspapers reported a positive response from the Peoples Democratic Party. Mufti Mohammad Sayeed applauded the Election Commission as well as the prime minister. He then added: 'The people of Jammu and Kashmir will have their right for the first time, to elect a chief minister through their elected representatives— and the Delhi Darbar will have no say in it.' (*The Times of India*, 30 September)

The meeting with the deputy commissioners of Udhampur and Kathua—these two districts were also in the third phase—was on 28 September. Udhampur had some pockets of militancy to be specially looked after, as well as polling stations for Kashmiri migrants.

By the 29th Rao was back in the Valley to not only oversee the elections, but specifically to tether the 'SOG'/ 'STF' to police lines.

His first stoppage was Avantipur, where he wanted to get a copy of the list of members of the 'SOG'/'STF' posted in Pulwama district. What was given to him was only a list of the force attached to Avantipur camp. There were two other camps in Pulwama district the lists of which were to be obtained from the DIG, Anantnag. Rao went to Anantnag and requested the DIG for a comprehensive list of the 'SOG'/'STF' in Pulwama and Anantnag districts. He was promised this but nothing happened. The following morning request and promise were repeated. During lunch on the 30th the deputy inspector general unblushingly changed position and told Rao he could get the list from the inspector general, Srinagar, whose permission he would need if Rao wished to visit the camps. Rao delivered a written ultimatum requiring the list by 4 p.m., failing which consequences would follow. Rao spoke to Chatterjee and then to me on phone. I contacted the chief secretary and told him the inspector general would have to be suspended. Malhi promised the list, and the word went down to Rao through Chatterjee. By 5 p.m. the list was given to Rao, and he saw to it that the entire 'SOG' in the two districts was confined to barracks. He virtually took a roll-call. He had quite ruthlessly accomplished his mission, or so we thought.

Rao, however, dug up an almost equally important issue. A brief mention has been made about road opening parties, essentially armed spearheads in militancy-ridden areas to allow free access to polling parties, their security, observers, and most of all, voters. On the 29th the deputy inspector general, Anantnag, advised Rao to request the army for all the road opening operations in Pulwama and Anantnag. In the meeting with the army commandant, Brigadier Bikram Singh, VSM, a brave and open-faced Sikh who had miraculously recovered after taking a full burst from a militant's AK-47—the BSF commandant and the deputy inspector general, Brigadier Singh suggested selective ROP by the army on major roads, the remaining army personnel being deployed at strategic points for area-domination. It was this domination which would give confidence to the voter to turn up at the polling stations. The deputy inspector general, however, insisted on across-the-board army ROP. Brigadier Bikram Singh then requested Rao to visit his office so he could be privy to the army plan. Rao did so, was given a briefing on the army plan, and then spoke to me on phone.

After consulting on phone the 15 Corps Commander, Lt. Gen. Patankar, a very pleasant and efficient general with the air of a university professor, I told Rao that we agreed with the army commandant's plan. At the commission we had begun to realize that getting the army fully absorbed in ROP and removing the army's area-domination, so that the 'SOG'/'STF' would be free to filter out voters expected not to vote for the ruling party, were part of a design to rig the elections in Anantnag and Pulwama. By all accounts the ruling party had fared badly in the first two rounds, and had to recoup in Anantnag and Pulwama if it was to be returned to power. But was it only the National Conference which at this stage was alarmed at free-wheeling elections, unpredictable results and the possibility of uncomfortable elements in the government-to-be? According to the *Indian Express* of 24 April 2003, Deputy Prime Minister L.K. Advani admitted in a Rajya Sabha debate: 'a few bureaucrats in Delhi had wanted him to influence the recently held elections in Jammu and Kashmir', but he had resisted this. Were some officers in the home ministry, therefore, trying to play Almighty in Pulwama and Anantnag through the local police?

On the 30th Rao also inspected the counting centre at Anantnag, which was by a river. Between him and the army commandant, they ensured the sanitization of the area.

The third phase of the poll was on 1 October, and the first thing I saw in the *Asian Age* (Delhi edition) was a photograph showing two surrendered militants in front of a shop in Anantnag. I spoke to Rao on phone, and he got a fax copy of the photograph, showed it to the deputy inspector general and wanted to know who they were. He then visited the army commandant and asked him whether the two surrendered militants were under army control. The photograph was shown to the other army officers, but no-one seemed to recognize them. Rao then decided to visit the barracks where such ex-militants were confined. The commandant agreed, but before going there he covered his own face—he had been attacked before, as mentioned earlier, and was still a prime target for the militants though carrying a hole in his chest. He asked Rao whether he would like to go with him in his jeep or in a separate vehicle. Rao fancied the distinction of travelling with him.

In the barracks, the surrendered militants in civvies seemed as harmless as anybody else. There was a roll-call, and the officer directly in charge of them confirmed that the two ex-militants in the *Asian Age* photograph were with him. They had been photographed on security duty during the chief minister's visit two days earlier. Towards the end of August the Jammu and Kashmir government had been directed to confine special police officers in secure camps, but not the army. It was among special police officers that ex-militants had been inserted, and it did not occur to the commission that the army had also got its quota.

Sometime later there was a phone call that the poll was being disturbed in a village 20 km from Anantnag. This was confirmed with the army commandant who volunteered to take Rao there. In the village they found two militants with rifles sitting in a teashop. They were promptly arrested.

The electronic media enjoyed itself reporting high turnout in the chronically militancy-affected districts of Pulwama and Anantnag. Vikram Chandra was in the middle of it. In Kathua and Udhampur attention diverted to the terrorist killing of six bus passengers near an army camp in Hiranagar.

The turnout of voters was 42.6 per cent.

Repoll was necessary in one polling station of 65-Kathua constituency because of the mechanical failure of an EVM. Four polling stations of 46-Pahalgam constituency of Anantnag district saw repolling because of electoral malpractices.

At the conclusion of the third phase there were not enough volunteers from among the polling officers from Uttar Pradesh for duty in the fourth stage at Doda. So all the polling personnel from Uttar Pradesh were sent home on 2 October.

In recounting the events, one has had little time to look at the human aspects of the deputation of polling parties from outside the state. It is necessary to appreciate some of these through a few examples.

Muhammad Faiyaz Khan, an assistant teacher in a primary school in Aligarh, was put in an air force plane and was pleasantly surprised to be in Srinagar within an hour. He was in a Border Security Force camp and took to it. He rather liked being issued raw chicken which he could cook his own way. He was assigned to Latifabad and had to walk 25 km either way. Polling was peaceful. In the second stage he did incident-free duty at Lasjanbee. In the third phase his work was at Fulwaya. He called home, saying he would return on 2 October and learnt his wife had had a heart attack, been admitted to a medical college and then discharged. He was quite melancholy as a result, but there was dinner at 6 p.m. to think about. He went outside the camp to relieve himself and was hit in one eye by a bursting grenade. He was flown to All India Institute of Medical Sciences, Delhi, and given the best and most urgent treatment, but he lost his eye. He was monetarily compensated on as generous terms as possible. Noor Mohammad, my colleagues and I will always regret the loss of his eye.

Jamal Ahmed Khan from Barabanki district had done duty in 1996. He was deployed at Bangdhar in Kupwara and was surrounded by Pakistanis on three sides. He was put through the ritual of firing from the other side and taking shelter in the bunker. Though not in love with the semi-cooked food and long steep climbs to the polling station, he was prepared to go again.

Muhammad Ashiq, an Urdu teacher from Meerut, volunteered for the extra money to marry off his sister.

Mohammad Yamin Raeen, chairman, Uttar Pradesh Urdu Development Committee, did duty in Belaboniar, Gandharbal and Noorabad. With no STD facilities, he and his colleagues communicated with their families through newspapers like *Amar Ujala* and *Dainik Jagran*. After being with the Border Security Force he thought a teacher's job was the easiest and a fauji's the most difficult. He felt that Kashmiris were caught between militants and military, and politicians on both sides were responsible for the mess.

Likewise the Punjabis left for home on 2 October, but by bus and not by air. Getting enough volunteers among them had not been easy. Ludhiana employees agitated and the district quota had to be scaled down. On the other hand, Hoshiarpur district, thanks to Deputy Commissioner Kirandeep Singh, contributed 300 volunteers. As Gurjit Singh Cheema, chief electoral officer of Punjab and author of the *Forgotten Mugals* commented: 'Seasoned government employees—like old soldiers—seldom volunteer, but if detailed for such "voluntary" missions the majority accept, or protest only half-heartedly.'

To quote Gurjit again: 'Later it was learnt that the volunteers were in high spirits when they left Hoshiarpur. The buses drove off to the sound of *Jaikaras* (battle-cries); they left in the spirit of *jehadis* leaving on a crusade in the cause of Democracy (which is one of the sacred totems of the times); but unfortunately their courage was Dutch courage, reinforced by the well-known power of *desi sharab* and Indian Made Foreign Liquor (IMFL). Wiser after the event, instructions were sent to all the DCs over telephone to appoint responsible group leaders for each bus, and enjoining the need for sobriety, and repeating the warnings found on every excise liquor bottle, that the consumption of liquor was injurious to health. Unfortunately throughout the "campaign" the conduct of the Punjab contingent remained marked by its excessive devotion to Bacchus. The Jammu and Kashmir authorities were shocked, and maybe a little awed. They had never seen such warriors before. The parties proceeding to Poonch and Rajauri were required to break their journey at camps at or about Jammu. The next morning the local officials had quite a time rousing the weary travellers and getting them into their buses again. Many of them were clearly nursing heavy hangovers.'

But alas it was not just fun and humour. There was a tragic side to the deputations. Kuldip Singh, a 54-year-old Hindi teacher, was found dead in his seat when the bus arrived in Jammu. He had had a massive heart attack. Mandeep Singh, teaching science near Phagwara, had enthusiastically volunteered though suffering from fever. He fought off suggestions from family members that he request to be excused, and was excited about going to Jammu and Kashmir. He got worse and a couple of days later was evacuated by helicopter to the Post Graduate Institute of Medical Education and Research, Chandigarh, but died after three days. The others who did not return were Amrik Singh, junior assistant, Audit Office, Amritsar, Jiwan Prakash, lecturer, Government Senior Secondary School, Jullunder and Kuldeep Singh (who succumbed to injuries sustained in a grenade attack). In addition Suraj Prakash, junior engineer from Hoshiarpur, fell from the first floor of the building in which he was staying, broke his spine and became paraplegic. He too got hurt answering the 'call of nature'.

All fatal Punjab casualties attracted the maximum

monetary compensations, and were also given state funerals. But Gurjit and my colleagues and I will ever bear the guilt of unwittingly having sent them to a premature death. For Suraj Prakash it was worse than death.

Media focus in Doda was on the spectacular flying-in of polling parties to remote polling stations and the crossing of logistical hurdles. Fifty-two per cent of the electors voted.

There was a repoll in one polling station of 53-Doda constituency on account of a mechanical failure in an EVM. Repoll was also necessary in another polling station of the same constituency as well as one polling station of 51-Kishtwar constituency on account of electoral malpractices.

The National Conference won 28 of the 87 seats, securing all three seats in Poonch and four of the five seats in Kupwara. The Congress came second with 20 seats taking three out of five seats in Kathua district and eight seats out of thirteen in Jammu district. The Peoples Democratic Party followed with 16 seats. It took four out of six seats in Pulwama and six of the ten seats in Anantnag. Independents numbered 13. One of these was a rebel People Conference candidate.

24

10 October to July 2003—
Afterwards

How did people perceive the elections? The Institute of Social Sciences, New Delhi, which had its own election watchers and mentioned unusual features like poll violence and heavy security deployment, nevertheless concluded that there had been a free and fair poll.

Rekha Chowdhary and Yogendra Yadav in the *Indian Express* of 9 October had rated the 2002 Jammu and Kashmir polls the 'fairest of them all'. And in 'Elections 2002: Implications for Politics of Separatism' in the *Economic and Political Weekly* of 4 January 2003, Rekha Chowdhary and Nagendra Rao had this to say: 'Placed in the context of the gradually extending democratic space on the one hand and the mounting pressures upon the separatist politics, on the other, the assembly election of 2002 provides important insights into the political psyche of Kashmir at the present juncture. This is more so because in many ways, the current election can be seen as a reversal of 1987 assembly elections which by eroding the democratic space had became catalyst for extension of separatist politics. Underlying the extreme popular response after that election were two commonly shared perceptions. First, that electoral politics would never give a fair chance to Kashmiris to represent themselves; and secondly, that there was no linkage between the political preferences of people and the governments that are formed in the state. The recently concluded assembly elections have altered these popular perceptions. This election has brought about a change in the regime through the popular verdict and to that extent it has become instrumental in providing a linkage between the people and the government.'

In the *Economic and Political Weekly* of 11 January the Coalition of Civil Society in 'Kashmir Assembly Election: How free and fair?' was of the view that the election had been 'flawed both in conception as well as in its conduct'. But the article is highly polemical, starting off with 'An election cannot be considered "free and fair" if the electors are denied their fundamental right to live in dignity and to exercise their civil liberties.'

It is unhappy with there having been no intensive revision of the electoral roll for a long time. Militancy and terrorism can be blamed for this but special measures made up for it, as has been amply explained earlier.

The other point made is that while there were more people in the Valley than in Jammu according to the 2001 census, there were less voters. In a census all heads are counted wherever they are found on a particular day, and the tally includes foreigners, Kashmiris, other Indians, civilians, soldiers, policemen, paramilitary forces, tourists . . . Voters, on the other hand, are a very restricted lot— normal residents of a place/area, above 18. It is evident that continued insecurity in the Valley has disrupted the process of enrolment of new voters. But in the fourteen years of annual summary revision of electoral rolls any voter left out only had to present an application. Finally, in the absence of age-group census profiles, it is not possible to comment on whether there has been a suppression of the official voter strength in the Valley or an inflation of it in Jammu.

The article alleged that the 'SOG'/'STF' had coerced voters to vote in all stages but the third one. It also said that the Election Commission had initially confined this force to the police lines, but had lifted the ban before polling to reintroduce it in the third stage under public protest. The fact is that the initial instructions were that this force would not operate on its own but only with the army and paramilitary forces. It was confined to barracks before the third stage when tying it to the army or paramilitary forces was not enough, and some elements in the state police were determined to misuse it to rig the elections. The question was not forcing voters to vote, but filtering out voters of the opposition parties. The National Conference won all three seats in Poonch district and four of the five seats in Kupwara district. If the 'SOG'/'STF' had done some mischief behind the back of the army and paramilitary forces, we will never know. There were also references to poll violence as instances of coercion by militants. Evidently prevailing conditions were not ideal for elections but in greater part, the state electors disregarded militants and voted in large numbers. It must be admitted, however, that the Election Commission, in the process of events, missed the significance of the thoroughly televised encounter—televised at the initiative of the police—in Srinagar, the night before and the whole morning of the day of poll. As the commission saw it, the purpose was to frighten people away from the polling stations, and help the ruling party win some seats.

Something more sobering was contained in the findings of a post-poll survey by Lokniti: Institute for Comparative Democracy.

I have referred to this report, showing nearly 80 per cent

of the people questioned in the Valley wanting a reunited and independent Kashmir. There were other parts to it. Of those questioned in the Valley, 39.6 per cent did not trust the Election Commission at all, 21.6 per cent trusting it 'somewhat', and 6 per cent a 'great deal'. 32.9 per cent were in the category of 'don't know'. 27.5 per cent in the Valley agreed with the proposition that Kashmir was never a part of India, and 43.7 per cent emphatically agreed with it. Again 26.6 per cent and 51.9 per cent agreed and 'strongly' agreed respectively with the proposition that the Kashmir problem could not be resolved through elections. Such basic polemical biases could not but have, at least partly, rubbed off on the Election Commission which, as pointed out in an earlier chapter, had always been considered an intrusion into the sovereignty of the State of Jammu and Kashmir.

The comments of the Pakistan government were flamboyantly negative and unembarrassedly inaccurate. Here are a couple of them:

> There has been a maximum of 10 per cent turnout in some areas, while in most parts it was as low as two per cent.

> —President Parvez Musharraf,
> 23 September 2002

> The people of Kashmir have rejected those elections. They are being coerced and forced to participate. We know from past experiences what kind of elections they were. What happens in the present exercise, we will get to know as the process goes on.

> —Aziz Ahmed Khan, Foreign Office spokesperson,
> Islamabad, 16 September 2002

But they were polemically consistent with those before the elections as well as with Pakistan's insistence on a plebiscite. A typical pre-election comment was:

> The Indians have held such farces of elections many times before. Regardless of the drama they (the Indians) would like to enact, that is no substitute for giving them (Kashmiris) a choice of joining Pakistan or India.
>
> —Maj. Gen. Rashid Qureshi, Military Regime Spokesperson, Rawalpindi, 10 August 2002

The Kashmir and later the Gujarat elections had visibly pleased the Indian liberal middle class and media as well as the international community and media, and had made the Election Commission a universally recognized institution. There was a flood of diplomatic visitors. Eminent judges and parliamentarians from other countries, who would normally have confined their visits to Parliament or the Supreme Court, also dropped in because they considered the commission was one of the most respected institutions in the land.

In deference to the commission's sensitivities regarding international observers, foreign diplomats made no public pronouncements on the elections but were very appreciative of the commission in private conversation. The US State Department, however, made the following press statement:

> The United States welcomes the successful conclusion of elections in Jammu and Kashmir. Prime Minister Vajpayee's personal commitment to making them transparent and open was a critical factor that helped to take the process forward. We hope that this will be the first step in a broader process that

will bring peace to the region. We applaud the efforts of the Indian Election Commission and commend the courage of candidates and voters who chose to participate despite violence and intimidation. The Kashmiri people have shown they want to pursue the path of peace.

And the Gujarat election—for which the Election Commission was equally applauded—also over, I was invited to lunch by the European Union in which its president, the ambassador of Greece, presented the Election Commission with a copy of Pericles' Funeral Oration which eulogized the inherent strength of democratic Athens as against the brittleness of totalitarian Sparta. I was one of the three—the other two being Mgr. Carlos Filipe Ximenes Belo, former bishop of Dili (East-Timor) and Mr Abdurahman Wahid, former president of Indonesia—invited by the French government to a symposium on 'Religion and Politics in Asia: Past and Present'. Finally, in quick succession I was selected for the *Business Week* magazine's Stars of Asia and Ramon Magsaysay Foundation's awards in 2003.

Did Pakistan try to sabotage the elections apart from ensuring the Hurriyat Conference's non-participation? Beginning July 2002 there was a spurt in infiltration across the international border, in violence and in security forces casualties. Some fifty *panches* and *sarpanches*, mostly National Conference adherents, were eliminated in the run up to the elections. There was a supporting poster campaign—even local Urdu newspapers were used—asking people to sever links with the National Conference and not to vote.

Though difficult to prove, this was obviously inspired by Pakistan. But not entirely. The *Indian Express* and the

Hindu of 16 June 2003 carried a report in which the Jammu and Kashmir police blamed six of its men for working in concert with militants to murder the then law minister Mushtaq Ahmed Lone and his brother Mohideen Lone in separate incidents in 2002. And many cases of the gunning down of innocent people by men in uniform are coming to light.

Epilogue

General Musharraf's statement that 'he will not permit any territory under Pakistan's control to be used to support terrorism in any manner' in the Islamabad South Asian Association for Regional Cooperation summit of January 2004 so swiftly thawed Indo-Pakistan relations as to generate immediate expectations. Some of these were a gas pipeline from Iran through Pakistan to India and increased Indo-Pakistan trade, each country giving the other most favoured nation status, within the penumbra of a common currency and a free trade area for the South Asian region.

The outstanding issues between India and Pakistan, namely peace and security, Jammu and Kashmir, Siachen, the Tulbul naval project, Sir Creek, terrorism, drug-trafficking, economic and commercial cooperation and friendly exchanges would be handled through a 'composite dialogue' beginning in February 2004.

The 'composite dialogue' has been in constructive progress but Pakistan would like to retain its reservation about clinching issues until a new Indian government is installed in Delhi after the current Lok Sabha elections.

The Indo-Pakistan rapprochement has made the Jammu and Kashmir political climate more clement. (It, of course, began with the converse—clean elections in Jammu and Kashmir in 2002 installing a government of the people's own choosing that instead of being Delhi's stooge had energetically predisposed India and Pakistan to come closer to each other.) On the state's horizon, what the common man sees is the possible surrender of militants, the reopening of the Srinagar–Muzaffarabad road—the present restriction of movement of the people of Pakistan-occupied Kashmir beyond Muzaffarabad, within Pakistan, only making the exchange of people between the two Kashmirs sweeter—the ultimate reunification of all territories in the old princely state of Jammu and Kashmir and the final resolution of the Kashmir problem.

Bibliography

Akbar, M.J., *Kashmir: Behind the Vale*, The Lotus Collection, Roli Books Pvt Ltd., New Delhi.

Anand, A.S., *The Constitution of Jammu and Kashmir*, Third Edition, Universal Law Publishing Co. Pvt Ltd., Delhi.

Bamzai, Prithvi Nath Kaul, *A History of Kashmir*, Metropolitan Book Co., Delhi.

Dasgupta, C., *War and Diplomacy in Kashmir: 1947-48*, Sage Publications, New Delhi.

Debate in Constituent Assembly on Part XIII—Article 289, Election Commission of India, New Delhi.

Eliot, Sir Charles, *Hinduism and Buddhism: An Historical Sketch*, Routledge and Kegan Paul Ltd.

Grover, Verinder, *The Story of Kashmir—Yesterday and Today*, Deep and Deep Publications, New Delhi.

Hassnain, Fida, *A Search for the Historical Jesus*: Gateway Books, Bath.

Jha, Prem Shankar, *Kashmir, 1947*, Oxford University Press, New Delhi.

Landmark Judgements on Election Law, Publication Division, Election Commission of India, New Delhi.

Lawrence, Walter R., *The Kashmir Gazetteer*, Shubhi Publications, Delhi.

Manual of Jammu and Kashmir Election Law (Seventh Edition), Department of Law, Government of Jammu and Kashmir (as amended up to March 2002).

Seshan, T.N., *A Heart Full of Burden*, UBS Publishers' Distributors Ltd., New Delhi.

Varadarajan, Siddharth, *Gujarat: The Making of a Tragedy*, Penguin Books, New Delhi.

Singh, Khushwant, *A History of the Sikhs*, Princeton University Press, Princeton, New Jersey.

Wakhlu, Khem Lata, *Kashmir Behind the White Curtain*, Konark Publishers, Main Vikas Marg, Delhi.

Wani, Gull Mohd., *From Autonomy to Azadi*, Valley Book House, University Road, Hazaratbal, Jammu and Kashmir.

Index